MIDI
for BEGINNERS

MIDRASH
for BEGINNERS

EDWIN C. GOLDBERG

A JASON ARONSON BOOK

ROWMAN & LITTLEFIELD PUBLISHERS, INC.
Lanham • Boulder • New York • Toronto • Oxford

Passages from *Genesis Rabbah* are reprinted with permission of the publisher from *The Midrash Rabbah — Vol. II*, edited by Dr. H. Freedman © 1951, published by the Soncino Press, Brooklyn, N.Y.

A JASON ARONSON BOOK

ROWMAN & LITTLEFIELD PUBLISHERS, INC.

Published in the United States of America
by Rowman & Littlefield Publishers, Inc.
A wholly owned subsidiary of The Rowman & Littlefield Publishing Group, Inc.
4501 Forbes Boulevard, Suite 200, Lanham, Maryland 20706
www.rowmanlittlefield.com

PO Box 317, Oxford, OX2 9RU, UK

Copyright © 1996 by Edwin C. Goldberg
First Rowman & Littlefield Edition 2004

British Library Cataloguing in Publication Information Available

Library of Congress Cataloging-in-Publication Data

Goldberg, Edwin C.
    Midrash for beginners / by Edwin C. Goldberg.
        p. cm.
    Includes bibliographical references and index.
    ISBN 1-56821-599-1 (alk. paper)
    1. Midrash — History and criticism. 2. Midrash rabbah. Genesis —
Introductions. 3. Bible. O.T. Genesis — Criticism,
interpretation, etc. 4. Joseph (Son of Jacob) in rabbinical
literature. I. Title.
BM514.G64 1996
296.1'4061—dc20   96-4385

Printed in the United States of America

For Melanie, Joseph, and Benjamin

Contents

Preface

If anything can be predicted for the next century, it is that the pleasure that comes from reading serious literature will continue to diminish in our society. Particularly with Jewish classics, advances in technology may help us access the great texts of the Jewish people on CD-ROM, but the joy that comes from careful study around a table is in ever-increasing jeopardy. It is ironic that scholarly works of Judaica are being published in great number, but there is all too little material that presents our sacred texts to non-scholars. In recent years, a few notable exceptions have been produced that effectively introduce the Talmud to people without experience in text-study. The goal of this work is to do the same for the Midrash, a sister genre to the Talmud that has not received the same attention.

Although I received an average religious school education at my Reform Temple in Kansas City, Missouri, my interest in the Midrash only began when I became a rabbinical student. In college I had majored in English Literature, and my first real introduction to classic Jewish texts was filtered through my appreciation for the great texts of Western civilization. I quickly realized that the works of classical midrash often reached the level of literary art in their close, sensitive reading of the Bible as well as in their evocative and emotive style. Understanding that the term "literary" carries both good and bad connotations in our society, as well as a lot of baggage in the intellectual community, I use the designation here simply to refer to a quality that does not pervade works of popular culture. In other words, the authors of such texts do not set out to record history or reinforce dogma or even simply to tell a story. Rather, there is a sense that the text they create responds to a consciousness of form and structure, thematic interplay, and an understanding of the balance between Truth and Beauty. It is to appreciate both the Truth and the Beauty of the biblical tale that inspires me to offer this present volume.

Acknowledgments

I am very grateful to have spent the last few years studying and teaching the selections from the Midrash that are presented in this book. I particularly wish to thank:

Arthur Kurzweil and Jason Aronson Inc., for producing this work.

My teachers of the Midrash: Professors Lewis Barth, Richard Sarason, and Marc Bregman of the Hebrew Union College-Jewish Institute of Religion, and Professors Nechama Leibowitz, Ze'ev Mankowitch, and Avidgor Shinan of the Hebrew University.

My Midrash students at the Isaac M. Wise Temple in Cincinnati, Ohio, and the University of Judaism in Los Angeles. In addition, the many individuals with whom I studied at Temple Israel of Hollywood.

I also wish to thank the Melton Centre for Jewish Education in the Diaspora, under whose auspices the conceptual underpinnings of this work were formed. I am also very grateful to Cheri Ellowitz Silver and Rabbi Philip Nadel for reading the manuscript, and to Beverly Israel and Michelle Kent for their technical assistance.

Finally, I thank my wife, Melanie, for all her support and guidance.

Introduction: Midrash

WHY THIS INTRODUCTION IS SO BRIEF

Nechama Leibowitz, the great contemporary teacher of Bible commentary, has warned against providing introductions when teaching Jewish texts. She understands that great works of literature best speak for themselves. Following her advice, this book presents only a brief introduction to the genre of midrash. In each of the following chapters you will come to know what is midrash by studying it instead of by my defining it. In the conclusion, there is provided an overview of the nature of the midrashic process in general and various midrashic works in particular. It is strongly recommended that this overview be consulted only *after* finishing the preceding chapters.

In the meantime, it is obvious that some working definition of midrash is needed before we begin. Suffice it to say that there are two general meanings of the term "midrash":

1. It can refer to a process of interpreting Scripture. According to this definition, any comment which is directly or indirectly related to

the Bible is midrashic. (There are even those who claim the term for the general process of commenting on any text.)

2. The term can also refer to a specific body of classical rabbinic commentary on the Bible, edited from approximately the year 200 of the Common Era (C.E.) to the ninth century. For instance, one can go to a well-stocked Jewish library and find in English translation such works as the Midrash to the Book of Genesis.

In this book, when referring to the process of midrash, the word will not be capitalized. However, when a specific midrashic commentary is discussed, then the word will be capitalized.

Hence, *Genesis Rabbah*, the primary midrashic collection we will be studying, will be referred to as the Midrash. In addition, when speaking of the authors of such classic documents, they will be referred to as the Rabbis or the Sages, to distinguish them from rabbis and sages of other eras, including our own.

WHY DO WE HAVE MIDRASH?

Often when we see a movie, we leave the theater with many unanswered questions. Why did the hero return to face mortal danger? Or, how did the detective know to ask the butler if he was left-handed? Such musings are an accepted part of the movie-going experience, but when it comes to reading ancient books like the Bible, we often assume that our difficulties in understanding the text, or accepting its message, are unique to our time. For instance, when Abraham is told by God to sacrifice his beloved son Isaac, we might think that our inability to grasp the meaning behind this request reflects our own age's more modern orientation.

And yet, even a casual look at classic midrashic works shows us that for two thousand years or more, people have struggled with the Bible. Even the great teachers of their time, the Rabbis, often could not or would not accept the text at its face value. Therefore, they created commentaries which addressed their own questions about the text and about the world in which they lived. For them, the heroes of the Bible were not only ancient ancestors but also contemporary role models wrestling with such basic dilemmas as confronting the temptation to sin and explaining why good people suffer.

A classic example of how the Sages of the Midrash "reread" the Bible with their own eyes is found in their treatment of the biblical story of Joseph. To the Midrash, Joseph is not merely an ancestor who was kidnapped and sold into slavery in Egypt, whereupon he rose to great power. Joseph also symbolizes every Jew who must decide between spiritual rewards and political passions, between identifying as a Jew or hiding one's faith, and between succumbing to sexual temptation or overcoming one's animal desires. Therefore, through their midrashic comments, the Sages created a portrait of themselves as well as a portrayal of Joseph. Indeed, we might say they also created a portrait of us.

The goal of this book is to introduce you to the genre of midrash by focusing on its treatment of Joseph. Although the message of classic midrashic works has been preserved and revered for centuries because they were written by great Jewish readers of the Bible, the artistry and pleasure of this medium has often been overlooked. As we will see, beyond its appeal as a religious document, the Midrash to the Book of Genesis (i.e., *Genesis Rabbah*), in particular, features humor, profound literary insights, and a wonderful ability to highlight the ultimate concerns of even contemporary readers.

Because, by definition, *Genesis Rabbah* is related to the Bible, many passages of the biblical Joseph narrative will be presented. In addition, it is a good idea to consult a translation of the Bible. The translation in this book is taken from the Jewish Publication Society of America's 1917 version. Although a newer translation is available from the same publisher, the older version is better for the study of midrash. This is because midrash often chooses to understand the biblical text in a very literal way, and the older translation presents the text as such. (From a modern biblical scholarship perspective, the older translation is inferior precisely because it is too literal.)

The translation of the passages from *Genesis Rabbah*, a particular midrash to the Book of Genesis (hereafter referred to as the Midrash), is taken from the Soncino edition of H. Freedman, published in 1951. Some slight changes have been made by me in order to reflect more accurately the Hebrew text or a particular manuscript version of the Midrash which appears more logical. The translation of the passage from the midrash to the Book of Exodus is taken from the Jacob Z. Lauterbach translation, first published in 1933. The translation of the talmudic passage (in the appendix) is by Jonathan Cohen.

Chapter 1

Joseph at Home

As any fan of Agatha Christie knows, the secret to solving a detective novel is to never overlook a clue, even an obvious one. For instance, imagine the following tragic scenario: on a clear, moonlit night, a young woman drowns in a canoe accident. When questioned, her boat companion claims he tried to save her but could not see her because it was too dark. Even a novice Hercule Poirot would know that something is fishy with his story. Obviously, his excuse for not saving her contradicts the fact that the moon provided plenty of light. Although such evidence may not convict him, his story makes him a suspect.

Two thousand years before Agatha Christie was born, there developed the tradition in Judaism of reading the Bible with the eyes of detectives. Naturally, the goal was not to identify criminals, but to glean new insights from the biblical text. Nevertheless, the process of paying close attention to every nuance of the Bible was not unlike a modern detective's preoccupation with every detail. For these ancient readers, the Rabbis of the midrash, Scripture often appeared like unbelievable alibis: the text simply did not make sense. Verses seemed to contradict each other, or were needlessly repetitive. While modern readers may look at such texts and conclude that more than one tradition was stitched together (somewhat sloppily, they might add), the ancient readers could not consider such a solution. They fervently believed that God wrote the Torah, through the aid of Moses, and that the rest of the Bible was inspired by the Divine Spirit. Therefore, scriptural irregularities were not seen as testaments to poor proofreading by the biblical editors. Rather, they became doorways into spiritual discoveries. The trick was to catch the problem and devise an insightful solution.

As mentioned earlier, the biblical narrative that is the focus of our study is the story of Joseph. In the Bible, chapters 37, 39–47 of the Book of Genesis relate the journey of Joseph from a young, spoiled favorite of his father to a mature prime minister of Egypt who triumphantly confronts his past. Although a good deal of Genesis is devoted to the story, the biblical text leaves out details that were considered vital by readers of Scripture, rabbinic and nonrabbinic alike. As we will see, the Midrash fills in such details as how Joseph looked, behaved, and in general got himself into trouble. But the first midrashic comments to chapter 37 focus on the type of problem discussed above, namely, what do we do when the Bible appears to contradict itself?

Consider this passage, from Genesis, chapter 37, verses 1 and 2:

AND JACOB DWELT IN THE LAND OF HIS FATHER'S SOJOURNINGS, IN THE LAND OF CANAAN. THESE ARE THE GENERATIONS OF JACOB. JOSEPH, BEING SEVENTEEN YEARS OLD, WAS FEEDING THE FLOCK WITH HIS BRETHREN, BEING STILL A LAD, EVEN WITH THE SONS OF BILHAH, AND WITH THE SONS OF ZILPAH, HIS FATHER'S WIVES; AND JOSEPH BROUGHT EVIL REPORT OF THEM UNTO THEIR FATHER.

After a casual reading, the message of the above verses may appear clear and basically unproblematic. Joseph is introduced as a young man who works in the field but also finds time to tattletale on his brothers. In classic biblical style, the Torah does not waste a lot of time providing detailed descriptions of Joseph or the surrounding countryside; indeed, the basic tension between Joseph and his brothers is already intimated after a few words. But to the ancient Rabbis who composed our Midrash on Genesis (i.e., *Genesis Rabbah*), the above verses were vexing. First of all, let us note the laconic style of the Bible: to say tantalizingly that Joseph brought back evil report about his brothers without specifying what he said is frustrating to many readers. From the biblical account, we do not know whether or not Joseph was telling the truth or spreading lies. We also do not know whether or not his father encouraged Joseph or warned him not to provoke the anger of his brothers.

Beyond the interest in knowing more details, the Midrash is also troubled by an apparent contradiction in the text. The chapter begins by stating that the generations of Jacob will be discussed, and then immediately jumps to the story of Joseph.

Look at the comment that *Genesis Rabbah* makes concerning this problem:

Rabbi Samuel ben Nahman commented: THESE ARE THE GENERATIONS OF JACOB: JOSEPH. Surely Scripture should say, THESE ARE THE GENERATIONS OF JACOB: Reuben [i.e., Jacob's firstborn son]? The reason [why Joseph instead is mentioned] is this: . . . as the former's mother was childless [for many years], so was the latter's; as the former's mother had difficult labor, so did the latter's . . . as the brother of the former hated him, so did the brothers of the latter; as the brother of the former sought to kill him, so did the brothers of the latter seek to kill him; the one was a shepherd and the other was a shepherd . . . the one emigrated from the Land [of Israel] and the other emigrated from the Land; the one took a wife outside the Land, and the other took a wife outside the Land . . . the one went down to Egypt and the other went down to Egypt . . . the one died in Egypt and the other died in Egypt . . . the bones of one went up [from Egypt] and the bones of the other went up. (*Genesis Rabbah* 84:6)

This midrashic comment features an opinion by Rabbi Samuel ben [son of] Nahman, a teacher who lived in Palestine during the end of the third century of the Common Era. His views are featured often in the Midrash and Palestinian Talmud. (One difficulty in reading midrashic works is that we cannot be sure that the Sage mentioned in connection with a statement was the Sage who actually made the remark. Hence, our reliance on these attributions will be limited to occasional comments concerning the background of the putative authors.)

Rabbi Samuel begins by asking the obvious question: If we are to learn about the generations (or children) that come from Jacob, should not Reuben, the first born of Jacob, be mentioned first? After all, there are ten sons who are older than Joseph. Why are their stories not shared? The answer: because their stories are not as important. Joseph is the *spiritual* firstborn of Jacob. The two share a common love of God as well as lives that are tested with struggle and hardship. Their faith is forged through the furnace of many trials and temptations. Therefore, the Bible bypasses the other sons and immediately begins the essential tale of Joseph.

At least one modern biblical scholar, E. A. Speiser, suggests another solution to the problem: the words "THESE ARE THE GENERATIONS OF JACOB" in effect belong to the preceding chapter of Genesis, in which various geneological lists are presented. According to this interpretion, chapter 37 would actually begin with the words "JOSEPH, BEING SEVENTEEN YEARS OLD. . . ."

Even if he were alive today, Rabbi Samuel would not accept such an interpretation, because the tradition presents the first part of the verse together with the remainder, and an Orthodox Jew is not allowed to edit the biblical text or change prevailing tradition. According to the Midrash, Jacob and Joseph should be associated with each other because Joseph is existentially Jacob's firstborn son. Such an approach reflects the general tendency of the Bible to relate stories in which a younger son merits the blessing of the father because his behavior earns the blessing. As someone once observed, in the Bible, it is never a good idea to be the firstborn son.

To very careful readers of the biblical text, there is also another problem in the above verses. "JOSEPH, BEING SEVENTEEN YEARS OLD, WAS FEEDING THE FLOCK WITH HIS BRETH-REN, BEING STILL A LAD . . ." declares the Bible. The Midrash sees an apparent problem in the repetitive information about Joseph. If we already know that he is seventeen years old, why do we also learn that he is still a lad? When we remember that, to the ancient Rabbis, the biblical text was perfect, then we cannot simply say that the Bible is being redundant. There must be some reason for the repetition.

The problem is further complicated when we realize that the Hebrew word for lad, *na'ar*, is sometimes used in the Bible to describe a very young child. For instance, in Exodus 2:6, the infant Moses is called a *na'ar*. Can the Torah really mean that Joseph was a baby? Here is how the Midrash responds:

JOSEPH, BEING SEVENTEEN YEARS OLD. . . . He was seventeen years old, yet you say, BEING STILL A LAD! It means, however, that he behaved like a boy, pencilling his eyes, curling his hair, and lifting his heel. (*Genesis Rabbah* 84:7)

The anonymous Sage cited is not prepared to say that Joseph acted like an infant, but it is suggested that Joseph's behavior was childlike, playing dress-up and even being girlish. (Later, when Joseph is in Egypt, we will see that such behavior invites more trouble.) With its comment, the Midrash begins to paint a portrait of Joseph that is far from perfect. Already there is a hint that Joseph's behavior is, in part, responsible for the suffering that soon visits him. This theme is developed more in the next midrashic comment, which addresses the biblical declaration, "AND JOSEPH BROUGHT EVIL REPORT OF THEM UNTO THEIR FATHER."

AND JOSEPH BROUGHT EVIL REPORT OF THEM. . . .
Rabbi Meir said: [He told Jacob]: Thy children are to be sus-pected of [eating] limbs torn from the living animals. Rabbi

Judah said: They insult the sons of the bondmaids [Bilhah and Zilpah] and call them slaves. Rabbi Simeon said: They cast their eyes on the daughters of the country. Rabbi Judah ben Simon said: With respect to all three, "A just balance and scale are the Lord's" (Proverbs 16:11). The Holy One, blessed be God, rebuked him [Joseph]: Thou didst say, "They are to be suspected of eating a limb torn from a living animal," by thy life, even in the very act of wrongdoing they will slaughter ritually. . . . Thou didst say, "They insult the sons of the bondmaids and call them slaves, . . . [and you will be sold into slavery];" Thou didst say, "They cast their eyes upon the daughters of the land": [so now] I will incite a bear [i.e., Potiphar's wife] against thee. . . . (Genesis Rabbah 84:7)

Presented in the Midrash is a debate between various sages (the first three mentioned lived in Palestine during the second century of the Common Era) concerning the actual "evil reports" that Joseph brings home. To the sages, the description "evil" has a dual meaning. It not only implies that the reports were unfavorable, it also intimates that Joseph was not reporting fact. Certainly there is no place in Scripture itself where any of the three complaints can be supported (i.e., no one can prove that Joseph is lying), and yet the Rabbis gave these reasons in order to understand the biblical text. Indeed, the reason for these three suggestions becomes apparent in the later comment of Rabbi Judah ben Simon (fourth century), who points out that the punishments that Joseph will receive fit the crimes he has committed. His false and unpleasant words lead to actual and unpleasant realities: his brothers will kill a goat and use its blood to trick their father into believing that Joseph has been killed; Joseph will become a slave himself; and his master's wife will lust after him, leading to Joseph's imprisonment.

Essential to this comment, which is supported by having God speak to Joseph, is the fundamental rabbinic idea that no one is punished without reason. The Midrash offers a negative portrait of young Joseph, not only because the biblical text may suggest it, but because the Rabbis of the Midrash cannot conceive of a world in which the righteous suffer for no reason. The midrashic comments speak not only to Joseph's situation, but also to the Rabbis' lives. The first three sages mentioned lived in Palestine during the time of terrible persecution by Rome. As difficult as it was for them to believe that their suffering was produced by their own sins, such an answer was easier to accept than concluding that God had abandoned them, or even worse, that somehow God was unable to help them.

Especially since the Holocaust, the Rabbis' outlook has been impossible for many modern Jews to accept, but we should understand that the ancient Rabbis had little choice. They insisted that God was both benevolent and omnipotent, and in such a theological equation, the only explanation for personal or communal suffering was to believe that, with few exceptions, suffering came from sins.

In the case of Joseph, the suffering is not only seen as a response to the failings of an immature seventeen year old, it is also a vital factor in the dramatic process of maturation that will lead Joseph to become the wise and charismatic vizier of Egypt. As we also understand so well, the Rabbis know that such growth always comes with a price in personal pain.

When we meet Joseph in the Bible, it is hard to miss his obnoxious character. Postbiblical tradition, including some later midrashic works, gives Joseph the title "the righteous one" (or the "virtuous one"—in Hebrew it is the same word, hatsaddik) but it is clear that such an honorific title does not reflect Joseph's youthful days. To some extent, it is hard to blame Joseph. Like any extremely gifted child, he simply cannot handle his own genius. When he dreams that one day his family will bow down to him, the politic choice is to say nothing. But Joseph is too consumed by his own destiny to be still. Indeed, the dramatic impact of the story is greatly heightened by the distance between the dreamer and the dreams. Joseph, the smart-aleck nomad, loved only by his father, is so far removed from Joseph the Righteous, vizier of Egypt, that his telling of his dreams reflects extreme naivete more than malice or arrogance.

The logical response of the brothers is to hate him, which they especially do after his father gives Joseph an ornamented coat, signifying his special status. The Bible does not suggest that their hatred of Joseph reflects any fears that the dreams will come true. On the other hand, Scripture is more ambiguous when it comes to his father Jacob's response. After Joseph shares his dreams, the Bible declares, " . . . HIS BRETHREN ENVIED HIM; BUT HIS FATHER KEPT THE SAYING IN MIND." What does it mean to keep a saying in mind? Here is what the Midrash says:

BUT HIS FATHER KEPT THE SAYING IN MIND (Genesis 37:11). Rabbi Levi said: He [Jacob] took a pen and recorded the day, the hour, and the place. Rabbi Hiyya interpreted: HIS BRETHREN ENVIED HIM, BUT HIS [HEAVENLY] FATHER [i.e., God]—the divine spirit—bade him [Jacob]: KEEP THE SAYING IN MIND—the matter will be fulfilled. Rabbi Hama ben Rabbi Hanina [said]: Jacob did indeed foresee these events impending. Said he, "If my ledger has been scrutinized, what can I do?" (Genesis Rabbah 84:12)

The Rabbis mentioned here ("Rabbi" Levi—in fact he probably was not ordained—lived in third century Palestine, as did Rabbi Hiyya bar Abba and Rabbi Hama) never forget that the story is not only about Joseph; Jacob continues to be an important figure as well. Indeed, the story of Joseph is, in a real sense, the story of Jacob. Therefore, Jacob is not presented as an uninformed bystander. Like Joseph, he, too, senses the great future that awaits Joseph. He may not approve of Joseph's impolitic telling of his dreams, but he does not doubt that they will come true. After all, argue the Rabbis, the divine spirit would not leave Jacob in the dark. Although the vision of a father bowing down to his son must disturb him, Jacob's faith in God, attained after years of struggle, leads him to accept the future with equanimity.

When the Midrash presents Jacob complaining about the future, it is unclear whether he protests the idea of his bowing down to Joseph, or if he merely is saddened to think of all the suffering and hardship that will lead to the realization of the dreams. In either case, the Midrash displays a Jacob who understands the price one pays for being part of the divine plan. The glory involved does not wipe away the personal suffering that God's messengers often undergo.

The Bible continues by relating the conversation between Jacob and Joseph when the latter is sent to visit his hostile brothers:

AND ISRAEL [JACOB] SAID UNTO JOSEPH: "DO NOT THY BRETHREN FEED THE FLOCK IN SHECHEM? COME, AND I WILL SEND THEE UNTO THEM." AND HE [JOS-EPH] SAID TO HIM: "HERE AM I. . . ." SO HE [JACOB] SENT HIM OUT OF THE VALE OF HEBRON, AND HE CAME TO SHECHEM. (Genesis 37:13-14)

If one were writing a psychological analysis of Jacob's dysfunctional family, it would be important to consider the type of father who either is unaware of the level of animosity Joseph's brothers have for him, or is apathetic about it. Either way, a simple reading of these biblical verses presents a father who obviously jeopardizes the life of his beloved son by sending him alone to meet his brothers. Nevertheless, if we interpret the situation by way of the Midrash, then another view presents itself: Jacob, knowing full well that God somehow will protect Joseph, and that his sending Joseph is part of the divine plan, acts with the faith of a true believer. Consider the Midrash:

AND HE [JOSEPH] SAID TO HIM: HERE AM I. Rabbi Hama ben Rabbi Hanina said: Our ancestor [Jacob] was ever mindful of these words and was consumed with remorse. "I knew that thy brethren hate thee, and yet thou didst answer: HERE AM I." (Genesis Rabbah 84:13)

Once again, the sage Ben Hanina (third century, Palestine) portrays Jacob as a sad old man, aware of the heavy burden that service to
God entails. Jacob is not a thoughtless parent endangering his child;
he is a reluctant parent, knowing that his beloved son must leave him
because God wills it.

We should also note that Joseph's response, "Here am I," is not a
simple declaration of Joseph's presence. By saying these words, Joseph
is acknowledging that he will go wherever his father, and by extension, God, sends him, despite the risk. It is no accident that the very
same words are stated by Abraham in chapter 22 of Genesis when
God calls upon him to sacrifice Isaac. In other words, Joseph may still
be a naive and smug lad, but somehow he is already aware of the call of
destiny and its attendant dangers.

Next, the Midrash confronts a geographical problem in the biblical
text. We read thht Jacob sends Joseph out of the valley of Hebron.
Such a description is troubling, however, since Hebron is located in a
hilly region. Consider the Midrash:

SO HE SENT HIM OUT OF THE VALE OF HEBRON. But
surely Hebron lies on a mountain, yet you [i.e., Scripture] say,
OUT OF THE VALE OF HEBRON? Said Rabbi Aha: He
[Joseph] went to bring about the fulfillment of the deep designs
which the Holy One, blessed be God, had arranged between
Himself and His noble companion who is buried in Hebron [i.e.,
Abraham], as it says [earlier] in Scripture, "And [your descen-
dants] shall serve them [the Egyptians], and they shall afflict
them" (Genesis 15:13). (Genesis Rabbah 84:13)

At least to the Sages, the Midrash begins with an obvious question:
How can Hebron be associated with a valley? The answer, provided by
Rabbi Aha (since there are eighty sages in the Talmud and Midrash
given this name, exact identification is difficult, but he is probably a
Palestinian sage of the fourth century), is that the Hebrew words
"Emek Hebron" should be read literally (and playfully) as "the deep

designs of the noble friend." In other words, Abraham, a noble spiritual partner of Joseph, was told by God that one day his descendants would be slaves in Egypt. Joseph will now fulfill this promise by going to look for his brothers. At stake is more than a creative solution to a geographical perplexity. The Midrash also is reminding us that Joseph's life is linked to the manifest destiny of the Jewish people. Joseph may just think he is going to visit his brothers. In his naivete, he may not even be worried, although we have seen that his words, "Here am I," could lead us to conclude that he is aware of the dangers. In any case, the Midrash recognizes that this one act of Joseph's begins a vital chapter in the Jewish People's master story.

This idea is continued when Joseph arrives in Shechem and does not find his brothers. The Bible relates that Joseph meets a man who asks him what he seeks. Upon learning that Joseph is looking for his brothers, he directs him to Dothan. A modern reader may see the unidentified man as a plot device designed simply to continue the story. The Midrash, on the other hand, suggests that the man is a divine messenger, making sure that Joseph continues his quest. After all, if Joseph came to Shechem and received no word as to where his brothers had gone, we must believe that he would have turned around and headed home. Certainly it is doubtful that he would have continued north in the direction of Dothan. If Joseph had not met the "man" and had not continued his journey, then one thing is clear: most likely the kidnapping would never occur, and therefore Joseph would never be sold into slavery, he would never be thrown into jail, he would never interpret Pharaoh's dreams, he would never become prime minister, his brothers would never come to Egypt, their descendants would never become slaves, Moses would never lead them out, and God would never give them the Torah at Mount Sinai! To the Rabbis of the Midrash, the catalyst for such a cosmic chain of events only could have been a messenger of God.

When Joseph approaches his brothers, the Bible tells us that they conspired to kill him. The oldest brother, Reuben, pleads with them to spare his life. (Although one might argue that Reuben acts out of humanitarian concerns, it is also possible that he has an ulterior motive: Having fallen out of his father's favor when he slept with his father's concubine, Reuben hopes to restore his position by bringing Joseph back.) In the meantime, Joseph is placed into a pit. Actually, here is what the Torah states: "AND THEY CAST HIM INTO THE PIT—AND THE PIT WAS EMPTY, THERE WAS NO WATER IN IT." Once again, the Midrash cannot resist the opportunity to question the obvious repetition in the biblical text. Why must we be told that there was no water in the pit if we already know that the pit is empty? Thus, the Midrash:

AND THEY CAST HIM INTO THE PIT—AND THE PIT WAS EMPTY, THERE WAS NO WATER IN IT. There was indeed no water in it, but snakes and scorpions were in it. (*Genesis Rabbah* 84:16)

In this pithy remark, the Midrash not only answers its unstated question concerning the Bible's apparent redudancy; it also adds to the drama of the story. Joseph's life is still in danger. Indeed, only by the grace of God will he be spared a gruesome death. For, as later midrashic tradition makes clear, the only way he can survive the ordeal of the venomous pit is to rely on God's miraculous deliverance.

It is curious that Judah, the fourth oldest brother, is the one to suggest selling Joseph into slavery. Like the other brothers, Judah is troubled by Joseph's boasting and special status with Jacob. In addition, he may be interested in what Joseph's disappearance will mean for him. If Reuben, the eldest born, is not worthy of the blessing of the first born, and Simeon and Levi, the next two sons, also are undeserving, due to their inhumane butchery of the Shechemites (in a chapter preceding the Joseph story), then Judah knows that he stands to gain the most by Joseph's disposal. Nevertheless, he cannot condone bloodshed, and so he devises the selling of Joseph instead of his murder.

The deed being done, the brothers slaughter a goat and dip Joseph's torn ornamented coat into its blood. When the bloody coat is presented to their father, the brothers carefully avoid lying. "THIS WE HAVE FOUND," they declare. "KNOW NOW WHETHER IT IS THY SON'S COAT OR NOT." (Genesis 37:32) It appears that Jacob sincerely believes his Joseph is dead, based on his declaration, "AN EVIL BEAST HATH DEVOURED HIM; JOSEPH IS WITHOUT DOUBT TORN IN PIECES." (Genesis 37:33) And yet, as at least one extremely careful modern reader of the Bible (Robert Alter) has observed, there is something strangely artificial about Jacob's response. He goes through the motions of mourning, but even the formalities suggest an absence of true grief.

The Midrash reflects this ambiguity in its comment on verse 35, "BUT HE [JACOB] REFUSED TO BE COMFORTED [BY HIS OTHER SONS]."

A matron asked Rabbi Jose: It is written, "For Judah prevailed above his brethren" (1 Chronicles 5:2), and yet we read, "And Judah was comforted" (Genesis 38:12); while this man [Jacob] was the father of them all, and yet HE REFUSED TO BE COMFORTED! You can be comforted for the dead, he [the rabbi] answered, but not for the living. (*Genesis Rabbah* 84:21)

Our midrashic statement begins with a question asked of a noted teacher (Jose ben Halafta, born ca. 97 C.E., who was well known for his dialogues with Roman matrons) by a gentile Roman woman. The Midrash often uses this method to provide the motivation for the giving of a rabbinical answer. The matron, who is ironically learned in the Bible, poses a good question: If Judah, the leader of his brothers, allows himself to be comforted when his wife dies, then why can Jacob not take comfort after the death of Joseph? Although a simple solution might be to say that the death of children precludes the passing of grief, Judaism traditionally does not allow such an answer.

According to Jewish practice, no one, not even a parent, is allowed excessive mourning. In any case, the Midrash wishes to offer a radically different reading of the episode, reflecting the ambiguity of Jacob's mourning. According to Rabbi Jose, Jacob cannot mourn for Joseph because he knows that *Joseph is not dead.* Indeed, Jacob is more worried because he believes that Joseph must be alive and doubtlessly is suffering. This argument is derived from the Bible's earlier declaration that Jacob "kept the saying in mind," referring to Joseph's disturbing dreams. If Jacob truly believes in the predictions of Joseph, then he has no choice but to conclude that Joseph still lives. Nevertheless, his suspicion of his remaining sons' sincerity leads him to play the role of grieving father. Perhaps he intuits that his role is to act *as if* he believes them.

The final midrashic comment we will study in this chapter continues the exploration of Jacob's state of mind. As with so many of the midrashic comments, its genesis stems from an apparent problem in the biblical text. After learning that Jacob refuses to be comforted, once again the Bible declares, "AND HIS FATHER WEPT FOR HIM" (Genesis 37:35). The Midrash, as we will see, refuses to accept such a statement as a redundant description of Jacob's grief.

> AND HIS FATHER WEPT FOR HIM—this refers to Isaac [i.e., Jacob's father]. Rabbi Levi and Rabbi Simon discussed this. Rabbi Levi said: In his [Jacob's] presence did he weep, but on leaving him, he bathed, anointed himself, ate and drank. And why did he not reveal it to him? He argued: The Holy One, blessed be God, has not revealed it to him; am I then to reveal it to him? Rabbi Simon said: He [Isaac] wept with him [Jacob] because you must observe mourning rites with any person for whom you must mourn. (*Genesis Rabbah* 84:22)

The Midrash here reverses an earlier opinion (i.e., that Jacob knew Joseph was still alive) and suggests that it was Isaac who knew. Such a difference of opinion is not uncommon in *Genesis Rabbah*, which is, after all, a composite of various comments on the Torah. Indeed, in the comment above we find preserved a "discussion"—a disagreement may be a better term—between two teachers. The first one believes that Isaac pretends to mourn for his grandson, but all the while knows the truth. (No reason is given as to how Isaac knows that Joseph is not dead. Perhaps the fact that, if he were still alive, Isaac would be very old, leads Rabbi Levi to conclude that such an old man would possess great wisdom.) The second Sage, Rabbi Simon ben Pazzi (ca. fourth century Palestine), focuses on a basic question regarding mourning practice: According to Jewish tradition, grandparents need not mourn for their grandchildren, at least not in a formal way. However, from a midrashic understanding of the Bible, in which we learn that Isaac wept for his son, Jacob, we learn that grandparents, or anyone, can mourn with other mourners. Hence, while seeking to limit the obligation of mourning, Rabbi Simon appears to be expanding the opportunity for mourning to any caring family member or friend. Such an interpretation certainly reflects existential reality better than the artificial designations which our tradition mandates. After all, are there not times when a child loses a beloved grandfather or aunt and certainly deserves to wear the black ribbon associated with intense mourning? Tradition tells us that the ribbon is not for such a person, but we know that such grief does not always observe geneological boundaries.

If you are now wondering just how the Midrash jumps from the biblical narrative to a discussion of informal mourning practices, then you are beginning to understand the strange but interesting logic of the Rabbis. Such strange logic will only continue in the next chapter.

Chapter 2

The Judah Interruption

In 1967, the Beatles released an album entitled *Sergeant Pepper's Lonely Hearts Club Band,* and included was a song called "A Day in the Life." Actually, the song was an amalgamation of two songs, one by John Lennon and the other by Paul McCartney. The two composers, each having written half a song, decided to combine the two, creating a story about a man who kills himself in a car combined with the reflections of a man getting ready to go to work.

Ever since the song was released, Beatles fans have tried to unlock the meaning behind the words. Especially important has been the attempt to explain how the two seemingly contradictory parts of the song relate to each other. For example, although both parts feature a person traveling, in one part he is in a car, and in the other he is riding a bus. In addition to such problems, the learned Beatles fan knows that the song may reveal secret information about the supposed death of Paul McCartney in a 1965 automobile accident. (For years, rumors about his death were believed by many people.)

In the previous chapter we saw how the ancient Rabbis also wrestled with apparent inconsistencies in the biblical text. Like passionate Beatles fans, they approached such irregularities with the

17

desire to learn more from them about what they considered Truth. Obviously, in the latter case, such reality reflected the divine plan and not pop culture. Nevertheless, a comparison between the two phenomena is instructive, for in both instances the problem was due to different traditions that were juxtaposed together.

A perfect biblical example is found in the Joseph narrative itself. As we have seen, chapter 37 of the Book of Genesis presents the beginning of the Joseph story. In its concluding verses we learn that Joseph was sold into slavery and brought down to Egypt. The logical continuation of the story appears in chapter 39, where we learn what happens to Joseph in Egypt. But here the Bible appears to interrupt the Joseph story with an irrelevant digression, the story of Judah and Tamar. Indeed, for millenia, readers of the Bible have asked what chapter 38 is doing in the middle of the Joseph story. There are even modern scholars who suggest that the chapter either belongs before the Joseph story begins or after it concludes, and, in general, the chapter is viewed as an independent unit not associated with the Joseph story.

The Midrash takes another approach. First of all, since the Bible must be perfect in the eyes of the Rabbis, and therefore chapter 38 cannot be moved, the ancient Sages are forced to determine how Judah's story in this chapter relates to the interrupted Joseph narrative. Characteristically of the Midrash, the Rabbis waste little time in doing so.

"AND IT CAME TO PASS AT THAT TIME, THAT JUDAH WENT DOWN FROM HIS BRETHREN. . . ." (Genesis 38:1). Thus begins the biblical account, which follows directly after Joseph's being sold into slavery and being taken down to Egypt, where he is bought by Potiphar. The Hebrew phrase "AND IT CAME TO PASS AT THAT TIME" frequently appears in the Bible as a literary device for changing the scene. The Midrash, however, often interprets the words literally, as if the action described was coterminus with the action presented immediately before. Consider the comment of the Midrash:

AND IT CAME TO PASS AT THAT TIME..., Rabbi
Samuel ben Nahman began his sermon [by quoting from Scrip-
ture]: "*For I know the thoughts that I think toward you, saith the
Lord*" (Jeremiah 29:11). The tribal ancestors were engaged in
selling Joseph, Jacob was taken up with his sackcloth and
fasting, and Judah was busy taking a wife, while the Holy One,
blessed be God, was creating the light of the Messiah: thus [the
Torah tells us that] IT CAME TO PASS AT THAT TIME.
(*Genesis Rabbah* 85:1)

As in the previous chapter, the Midrash offers us the insight
of Rabbi Samuel, who apparently began a sermon on the subject
of chapter 38 of Genesis by quoting a verse from the prophetic
book of Jeremiah. It is not unusual for the Rabbis of the Midrash to
begin their remarks with a non-Torah verse, for they believed that the
entire Bible related to itself. They saw nothing illogical in postulating
that Jeremiah, living two thousand years later, could be speaking of
the present episode. The Jeremiah verse presents God declaring that
the divine mind has everything happen for a reason, a popular
rabbinic idea. In the case of Joseph and Judah, Rabbi Samuel argues
that at the very moment Joseph was sold into slavery, Judah decided to
leave his brothers and get married. As the biblical tale which follows
relates, Judah has three sons. After marrying a Canaanite woman
named Tamar, the first son dies. Following Jewish law, Judah then has
his second son marry Tamar, so that a child will be born with the
name of the deceased older brother. This second son refuses to fulfill
his duty and subsequently dies. When Judah refrains from placing his
youngest son in the same jeopardy, Tamar takes matters into her own
hands. She pretends to be a prostitute and tricks Judah, now a
widower, into sleeping with her. From this union two children will be
born. As is ironically customary in the Bible (though certainly not
according to normal custom), the younger son will inherit the birthright and, according to Jewish tradition, he will be the ancestor of
the Messiah.

Thus, at the same time that Joseph is sold into slavery, the Messiah is figuratively born. The next midrashic comment expands this point:

AND IT CAME TO PASS AT THAT TIME. . . . Before the first who shall enslave [the people Israel] was born, the last redeemer [i.e., the Messiah] was born, as it says, AND IT CAME TO PASS AT THAT TIME. (*Genesis Rabbah* 85:1)

All of a sudden, there is a connection between the Joseph and the Judah stories. Even before Joseph succeeds in Egypt, a success which ironically will lead to the slavery of his people, the seed of ultimate redemption is planted. In the Book of Exodus, we read that "there arose a pharaoh who knew not Joseph" (Exodus 1:8). Based on this verse, as well as a logical understanding of the biblical narrative, it is clear to the Midrash that the evil pharaoh who is "the first who will enslave Israel," has yet to be born. By recognizing that the Messiah had already been "ordered," the Rabbis are comforting themselves as well as any future readers. Living in a time of Roman persecution, their hope of redemption and God's eternal providence was vital to maintaining their spirits. Although it was difficult for them to understand how God would allow their suffering to occur, the alternative suggestion that God was not in control (and therefore, that there were other gods) was impossible for them to support. Hence, all they could do was hope that, since the Messiah was already waiting to arrive, the time would come soon.

If one is still skeptical concerning the place of chapter 38 in the Joseph story, the next comment seeks to respond.

AND IT CAME TO PASS AT THAT TIME. What precedes this passage? "And the Midianites sold him into Egypt" (Genesis 37:36), which is followed by AND IT CAME TO PASS AT THAT TIME; yet surely Scripture should have continued with, "And Joseph was brought down to Egypt" (Genesis 39:1)? Rabbi Leazar said: This was done in order to bring two passages of "descent" together. Rabbi Johanan said: In order to bring the

two phrases, "Know now whether or not," together. Rabbi
Samuel ben Nahman said: In order to bring the stories of Tamar
and Potiphar's wife into proximity, thus teaching that as the
former was actuated by a pure motive, so was the latter. For
Rabbi Joshua ben Levi said: She [Potiphar's wife] saw by her
astrological arts that she was to produce a child by him [Joseph],
but she did not know whether it was to be from her or from her
daughter. . . ." (Genesis Rabbah 85:2)

As we have seen before, the Midrash often presents a multiplicity
of interpretations, as if to say that the reader is responsible for
choosing which understanding is favorable. Despite the presentation
of three opinions, however, the above passage also reflects some
rabbinic unity. All three of the interpretations are built on the
presumption that chapter 38 is connected with the Joseph story. Let
us briefly examine where the interpretations differ.

Rabbi Leazar (short for Eleazar ben Pedat, died ca. 280 c.e.) argues
that the "descent" of Joseph into slavery (which is also geographically
accurate—one "goes down" to Egypt from the Land of Canaan) is now
reflected by Judah's descent from Canaan. In both instances, the same
Hebrew verb is used, meaning "to go down." The Midrash is making a
moral statement as well as a geographical observation: Judah's going
down is not only physical. His behavior with Tamar (not giving her a
husband) is seen by the Rabbis as unjust, as was his unwillingness in
chapter 37 to save Joseph and bring him home. Beyond its moral
comment, Rabbi Leazar's interpretation makes sense when we remember that, with the three oldest brothers disgraced in the eyes of
Jacob, and with Joseph out of the picture, Judah stands to become the
heir to Jacob's blessing, and so it is not so unnatural to learn more
about him. Making the reader wait a chapter to learn about Joseph is
also an effective method for inspiring the kind of suspense that
cinema cliffhangers give.

If we do not like Rabbi Leazar's comment, however, we need not
despair, for Rabbi Jochanan (a contemporary colleague) weighs in

with his own opinion. He argues that chapters 37 and 38 belong together because they both share an ironic phrase. In chapter 37, when the brothers bring back the bloodied coat to their father, they say, "KNOW NOW WHETHER IT IS THY SON'S COAT OR NOT," and of course the brothers know very well that it does belong to Joseph. In chapter 38, when Tamar has been accused of being a prostitute and becoming pregnant (in reality she has tricked Judah into sleeping with her and held on to his possessions as collateral), she uses the same words when confronting Judah. "KNOW NOW WHOSE ARE THESE" (Genesis 38:25) she declares.

Rabbi Jochanan recognizes that the same phrase used by Judah and his brothers in order to trick their father is now used by Tamar, who has tricked Judah. In other words, as the Rabbis of the Midrash liked to say, "what goes around comes around." What is so ironic is that both Judah and Tamar, through their deceit, are enabling God's plan to unfold. If Judah had not tricked his father, then Jacob conceivably might have gone to Egypt in order to rescue Joseph, and Joseph would never have become the powerful prime minister and thus never brought his starving family to Egypt, and the great story of slavery and redemption would never have happened. Similarly, had Tamar not tricked Judah, then the messianic line that will come from their union would never come to be.

The importance of executing God's plan is central to Rabbi Samuel ben Nahman's startling comment. According to him, just as Tamar's actions, although deceitful, are good, so is the behavior of Potiphar's wife! In the next chapter, much more will be said about this unnamed woman, but in order to appreciate Rabbi Samuel's argument, some background needs to be related here.

As chapter 39 develops, we see that Joseph becomes very successful in the house of his Egyptian master, Potiphar. We also meet Mrs. Potiphar, the libidinous mistress of the house who constantly tries to seduce Joseph. Her actions appear anything but virtuous. Not only does she harass Joseph and attempt to commit adultery with him; when Joseph refuses, she frames him and has Joseph sent to prison.

In the Midrash, the story becomes more complicated—and more interesting—when the Rabbis identify Potiphar and Potiphar's wife as the future in-laws of Joseph. The reason for this identification is that later, when Joseph marries, we read that his wife is Asenath, the daughter of Poti-phera (Genesis 41:45). Although the Bible does not suggest that Potiphar and Poti-phera are the same person, the Midrash likes the idea. In effect, Mrs. Potiphar becomes Mrs. Robinson from the movie *The Graduate*, falling in love with her daughter's eventual husband.

Contrary to what we would expect, Rabbi Samuel, and Rabbi Joshua ben Levi (also a contempory of the third century), see Mrs. Potiphar in a sympathetic light. Her behavior is not without merit, since she believes that either she or her daughter is fated to be with Joseph. Since the offspring of the union will be Ephraim and Manasseh, two of the tribes of Israel, the matter is very important. As it turns out, her Egyptian methods of divination are not perfect, and she mistakenly attempts to offer herself to Joseph, but the sin is made by a "pure motive," that is, her desire to help in the unfolding of the divine plan.

Whether we agree with Rabbis Samuel and Joshua, two important contributors to the Midrash, or with the statements of the other Rabbis, one conclusion is clear: all of them believe that chapter 38 belongs where it is. Interestingly enough, at least one modern literary scholar, Robert Alter (see For Further Study), finds convincing contemporary (i.e., literary) reasons to support the placement of chapter 38 in the Bible. In essence, this midrashic passage reflects not only a healthy rabbinic imagination but also a fine appreciation for the unity of Scripture, and even some sympathy for an oft-maligned Mrs. Potiphar. All of these characteristics will be evident in the next chapter as well.

Chapter 3

In Potiphar's House

JOSEPH SUCCEEDS

For many people today, it is not easy to identify with a seventeen-year-old shepherd, even one who is beloved by his father and owns an eye-catching coat. But when Joseph is brought to Egypt and forced to live by his wits and faith in God, then his character becomes much more contemporary. All of a sudden, Joseph is a model for each of us, as we are forced to make our way in an often hostile world. For Joseph, the specific setting is the house of Potiphar; his challenge is to please his master without forgetting his own identity or forfeiting his faith in the dreams he has witnessed. As we will see, his most immediate concern is to confront the dangers that await him in his new residence.

It has been said that, in the Joseph story, Joseph plays the role of "femme fatale." In other words, his good looks inspire self-destructive behavior from his admirers. While the biblical text does not support this claim (after all, it is Joseph who will suffer from the attentions of Mrs. Potiphar), the Midrash portrays Joseph not only as a victim of sexual harrassment, but also as an irresistably attractive young man who leads both male and female into trouble. The first victim is

Potiphar himself, as the Midrash will explain. But first, we begin with our biblical verse:

AND JOSEPH WAS BROUGHT DOWN TO EGYPT; AND POTIPHAR, AN OFFICER OF PHARAOH'S, THE CAP-TAIN OF THE GUARD, AN EGYPTIAN, BOUGHT HIM. . . . (Genesis 39:1)

Thus begins the saga of Joseph in Egypt. According to most translations, the Hebrew words *seris paro* are rendered as AN OFFI-CER OF PHARAOH. Nevertheless, in other contexts, the term *seris* means a eunuch (e.g., in the Book of Esther). This dual meaning of the term permits the following midrashic reading of our verse:

A EUNUCH (*seris*) OF PHARAOH. This intimates that he [Potiphar] was castrated, thus teaching that he purchased him [Joseph] for the purpose of sodomy, whereupon the Holy One, blessed be God, emasculated him. This may be compared to a she-bear who wrought havoc among her master's children, whereupon he [the master] ordered, "Break her fangs." In the same way we are taught that he bought him for the purpose of sodomy, but the Lord emasculated him. (*Genesis Rabbah* 86:3)

By arguing that Potiphar wanted to rape Joseph, the anonymous author of this midrashic comment succeeds in portraying the danger that young Joseph faces. He is alone, without rights, and at the mercy of his owner. And yet, behind the scenes, God is with Joseph, even in Egypt. The Midrash is not content to let such a fact remain in the background; therefore, the biblical text is deliberately misread so that Potiphar becomes a eunuch instead of simply an officer of Pharaoh. Contextually, his being a eunuch and being married does not make sense. Nevertheless, his *becoming* a eunuch serves the Midrash well, for Potiphar's emasculation is a direct result of his mischievous plans, and therefore his punishment supports a basic rabbinic belief in poetic justice. Also, although the Midrash may not intend it, Potiphar's condition makes his wife's lusting for Joseph a little more understandable, for obvious reasons.

In order to make its point, the Midrash employs a parable, in this case, a story about a family with a pet bear. Most likely, this reference reflects the contemporary environment of the Rabbis in Palestine, in which bears often provided such entertainment (for the Romans). The fact that a she-bear is mentioned (here representing Potiphar) may refer to his emasculation, but also may foreshadow Joseph's upcoming episode with Mrs. Potiphar.

The biblical text then informs us that God is with Joseph in Egypt. For the traditional reader of Scripture, such a statement makes sense. The following verse, however, is more difficult to understand. AND HIS MASTER SAW THAT THE LORD WAS WITH JOSEPH AND THAT THE LORD MADE ALL HE DID TO PROSPER IN HIS HAND. (Genesis 39:3)

If taken literally, these words suggest that Potiphar, an Egyptian idolator, somehow was able to recognize the divine presence hovering over Joseph. From a theological viewpoint, such a fact is puzzling, and from a literary perspective, such a quality is suspect. How could Potiphar see God and also understand what he saw? Consider the Midrash:

AND HIS MASTER SAW THAT THE LORD WAS WITH HIM AND THAT THE LORD MADE ALL HE DID TO PROSPER IN HIS HAND. Rabbi Huna interpreted in Rabbi Aha's name: He [Joseph] whispered [God's name] whenever he came in and whenever he went out. If his master bade him, "Mix me a drink of hot [liquor]," lo! it was hot; "Mix it for me lukewarm," lo! it was lukewarm. "What means this, Joseph!" exclaimed he; "Would you bring straw to Afrayim, or pitchers to Kefar Hananiah, or fleeces to Damascus, or witchcraft to Egypt—witchcraft in a place of witchcraft!" How long [did Potiphar suspect him of witchcraft]? Said Rabbi Huna in Rabbi

Aha's name: Until he saw the divine presence standing over him. Hence Scripture says, AND [WHEN] HIS MASTER SAW THAT THE LORD WAS WITH HIM. . . . (*Genesis Rabbah* 86:5)

The subject of this comment (probably by Huna bar Abbin of fourth century Palestine) is no less than this question: how does a non-Jew recognize the divine presence? We are allowed to see Joseph from Potiphar's point of view, and learning from this perspective, we encounter another side of Joseph. According to the Midrash, Joseph is a "*baal shem tov*" — a "master of the holy Name of God" — and uses his powers to effect simple bartending tricks. (How he became a master of the Name is not addressed.) Although the tricks may be mundane, they will help him impress his boss, a trait always important for Joseph. Naturally, Potiphar assumes that such magic must be the result of witchcraft and, perhaps with some humor, teases Joseph for, in effect, bringing coals to Newcastle. It is only then that Potiphar sees what most believers never see, the Divine Presence. His revelation leads him to respect Joseph all the more, leading the biblical text to declare, "AND JOSEPH FOUND FAVOR IN HIS [MASTER'S] SIGHT" (Genesis 39:4).

As a result of his gaining the favor of Potiphar, Joseph assumes control of the entire household. The biblical text is very specific on this point: "AND HE [POTIPHAR] LEFT ALL THAT HE HAD IN JOSEPH'S HAND; AND HAVING HIM, HE KNEW NOT AUGHT SAVE THE BREAD THAT HE DID EAT" (Genesis 39:6). According to the Bible, Joseph was powerful but with one limitation: Potiphar was responsible for his own food. There may be a logical explanation for this practice; perhaps Potiphar feared that Joseph the Hebrew might make his meal impure, or worse. (In the next chapter, Pharaoh's baker will be thrown in prison, and some commentators indicate that his crime was attempting to poison the king.)

In addition to a rational explanation for Joseph's limitation in service to Potiphar, the Midrash offers a more creative reading:

AND HE LEFT ALL THAT HE HAD IN JOSEPH'S HAND;
AND HAVING HIM, HE KNEW NOT AUGHT SAVE THE
BREAD THAT HE DID EAT. This is a euphemism [for Pot-
iphar's wife]. (*Genesis Rabbah* 86:6)

With one brief comment, the Midrash reminds us that Joseph and
Potiphar are not the only major characters on stage. The antagonist of
this part of Joseph's life is about to make her formal entrance, and the
fact that Joseph controls everything belonging to Potiphar—except
for Mrs. Potiphar—foreshadows the tense encounters to come. All of a
sudden, young Joseph is involved in an early version of *The Postman
Always Rings Twice*.

Viewed from the perspective of the entire Bible, the Joseph story is
certainly important, but the episode with Potiphar's wife is not a
major component. Far more vital is Joseph's betrayal by his brothers,
his eventual rise in Pharaoh's court, and his reunion and reconcilia-
tion with his family. But the encounter with Mrs. Potiphar has always
been a central focus for post-biblical commentary on Joseph. Indeed,
according to some scholars, Joseph's major test in life occurs when his
master's wife attempts to seduce him. Beyond his other struggles and
successes, it is argued, his ability to overcome sexual temptation
earned him the honor of being a patriarch. Certainly the fact that he
did not succumb to temptation is noteworthy, but the observation
may be irrelevant. After all, where in the Bible does it suggest that
Joseph was tempted in the first place?

Jewish tradition has awarded Joseph the title "Righteous One" or
"Joseph the Virtuous," as a reflection of his commitment to chastity. In
fact, early postbiblical reworkings of the Scripture, such as the *Testament of the Twelve Patriarchs*, present Joseph as a pillar of strength who is
not even tempted by Mrs. Potiphar's pleas. This is a Joseph who never
has a second thought about his loneliness or Mrs. Potiphar's attractive-
ness, or the advantages that might be gained by a discreet relationship.

Although such a view of Joseph may be comforting, it is also a little
boring and unbiblical. Part of the Bible's eternal charm is its presentation

of real people, not superhumans. It has been said in jest that one wouldn't want one's children to grow up to become like anyone in the Bible. Nevertheless, all of us reflect biblical characters to a great degree, for all of us are human. We *are* tempted; we *do* make mistakes; and we must suffer the consequences. Fortunately, Midrash *Genesis Rabbah* presents a Joseph that is very human. As we will see, he is quite tempted by Mrs. Potiphar, and the entire relationship between them is far more ambiguous than we might imagine. As we will see, there are those who even suggest that Joseph was a ready and willing partner.

JOSEPH SEDUCED?

Anyone who has fallen in love since the dawn of radio has probably had the following experience: you are enjoying the rapture of infatuation when a love song comes on over the airwaves. All of a sudden it seems that the words are speaking directly about you and your love. Even though the composer never met you, somehow it seems that your exact situation is being perfectly described.

A similar phenomenon often occurs in the Midrash. Specifically, a narrative in the Torah is connected with a passage from a later book of the Bible, such as a psalm or a selection from the Book of Proverbs. Although both texts appear unconnected upon first glance, the juxtaposition of them creates a counterpoint of meaning. The texts fill in the gaps and present a more complete narrative. The ancient Rabbis believed that such juxtapositions were more than creative reading; they reflected divine artistry at work.

A good example of the combination of Torah narrative with the Book of Proverbs is found in our Midrash. The narrative context is Joseph's being harrassed by Mrs. Potiphar, but the Midrash does not view the encounter as completely one-sided. In other words, Joseph, too, bears some responsibility for the amorous attentions of his mistress. As we will see, the Midrash claims that Joseph, in effect, "asked for trouble" because he made himself so attractive. They even find biblical support for this view, citing the fact that the Bible tells us that "JOSEPH WAS OF BEAUTIFUL FORM" (Genesis 39:6), followed by verse seven: "AND IT CAME TO PASS AFTER THESE THINGS, THAT HIS MASTER'S WIFE CAST HER EYES UPON JOSEPH." The ancient Rabbis see a connection between Joseph's behavior and his subsequent predicament. Before we see what they say, first consider the "song" which they relate to Joseph's tale. This passage is from the Book of Proverbs, and the context is fatherly advice to a son concerning keeping away from strange women.

For at the window of my house
I looked forth through my lattice;
And I beheld among the thoughtless ones,
I discerned among the youths,
A young man devoid of understanding,
Passing through the street near her corner,
And he went the way to her house;
In the twilight, in the evening of the day,
In the blackness of night and the darkness.
And, behold, there met him a woman
With the attire of a harlot, and a wily heart.
She is riotous and rebellious,
Her feet abide not in her house;
Now she is in the streets, now in the broad places,
And lieth in wait at every corner.
So she caught him, and kissed him,
And with an impudent face she said unto him. . . .
Come, let us take our fill of love until the morning;
Let us solace ourselves with loves.
For my husband is not at home,
He is gone a long journey,
He hath taken the bag of money with him;
He will come home at the full moon.
(Proverbs 7:6–13;18–20)

On first glance, there may be nothing in these words that reminds one of Joseph. Clearly, the man in this poem is seeking sin, and Joseph does not appear interested in such endeavors. Nevertheless, look at how the Midrash weaves the two passages together:

AND IT CAME TO PASS AFTER THESE THINGS (Genesis 39:7). . . .
   I discerned among the youths a young man devoid of understanding (Proverbs 7:7). This alludes to Joseph. He was devoid of understanding in that he slandered his brothers—is there any greater lack of understanding than this! *And behold, there met him a woman* (Proverbs 7:10), viz. Potiphar's wife; *With the attire of a harlot*—for Joseph; *And a wily heart*—toward her husband. *She is riotous and rebellious,* which means, she went about weeping. *Her feet abide not in her house,* but, *Now she is in the streets, now in the broad places,* etc., asking people, "Have you seen Joseph for me?" *So she caught him and kissed him*—AND SHE CAUGHT HIM BY HIS GARMENT (Genesis 39:11); *She looked impudently at him*—SAYING: LIE WITH ME (Genesis 39:11). Hence we read, AND IT CAME TO PASS AFTER THESE THINGS. (*Genesis Rabbah* 87:1)

The tacit message of the Midrash is that the biblical account, although certainly compelling, does not give the reader enough information. We want to know more about Mrs. Potiphar and we want to see the struggle that Joseph must endure, not only with his mistress but also with himself. The Proverbs selection may not actually be related to chapter 39 of Genesis, but the two narratives do complement each other.

If we consider the juxtaposition of the two passages, we see a Joseph who foolishly flirts with his would-be seducer. His lack of judgment already was manifest in his slandering of his brothers, a practice not only unethical but also dangerous. Likewise, his behavior toward Mrs.

Potiphar, although perhaps innocent in his eyes, led to her dangerous attraction to him.

The midrashic comment cited above presents Potiphar's wife inn curious way. She is not the self-assured maneater that most of us usually picture when we read about her. Instead, she appears lovesick, frantic with lust for the beautiful Joseph and unable to think of anything else. (Remember the earlier comment that Joseph is the *femme fatale* of the story.) The motif of a distraught Mrs. Potiphar is not unique to *Genesis Rabbah*. For instance, in a much later midrashic work, the Book of *Yashar* (ca. 16th century, Italy, but reflecting earlier midrashic material), Potiphar's wife is portrayed as a desperate woman who is controlled by her passion for Joseph. When her female friends ask her what is wrong, she invites them to meet Joseph, whereupon they, too, are stunned by his beauty. (The women actually drop the knives they are holding and cut themselves without realizing it, so attracted are they to Joseph.)

Returning to *Genesis Rabbah*, it would seem that Joseph is not to blame for his misfortune. After all, can he help ⅝t that his beauty attracts unwanted attention? And yet, the Midrash generally reflects a worldview which states: If you are being punished, it is because you deserve it. In other words, Joseph's eventual imprisonment cannot be accepted by the Rabbis as a fluke of fate. They are much more comfortable with a world in which misfortune has a reason, even if such an outlook is of little comfort to the sufferer. Therefore, the Midrash seeks to prove that Joseph somehow deserves his punishment.

When it comes to Joseph's role in the Mrs. Potiphar affair, the Midrash has little trouble finding proof of Joseph's guilty behavior. They simply consider the biblical report of Mrs. Potiphar's interest in Joseph in context with what the Bible says immediately before.

AND IT CAME TO PASS AFTER THESE THINGS, THAT HIS MASTER'S WIFE CAST HER EYES UPON JOSEPH; AND SHE SAID: "LIE WITH ME" (Genesis 39:7). What precedes this passage? "And Joseph was of beautiful form, and fair to look upon" (Genesis 39:6). [What is the connection between these verses?] It may be illustrated by a man who sat in the street, pencilling his eyes, curling his hair and lifting his heel, while he exclaimed, "I am indeed a man." "If you are a man," the bystanders retorted, "here is a bear; up and attack it!" (*Genesis Rabbah* 87:3)

According to the Midrash, Joseph was not in trouble because of his natural good looks. He cultivated them (to the point of excess) and therefore Mrs. Potiphar pursued him. Joseph is compared to a dandy who cares for nothing but physical appearance; his "reward" is Mrs. Potiphar, here characterized as a bear (earlier it was her husband).

When we remember that the Rabbis cited in *Genesis Rabbah* lived during Roman rule, we can appreciate their concern for narcissistic passions, which in their eyes was a form of idolatry. To the Rabbis, Joseph was too full of himself and the time had come for the type of challenge that either destroys or refines an individual. Although God may have a divine plan that will be fulfilled, *we must not forget that for Joseph, everything is new, and his future far from certain.* His encounter with Potiphar's wife might be the end of him and his haunting dreams of glory.

And yet, it is possible that a part of Joseph wanted to be tested. Having survived his initial setback, perhaps he wished to see how bad things could get. Consider the next midrashic comment:

AND IT CAME TO PASS AFTER THESE THINGS [*debarim*]. . . . There was some indulging in reflections there. By whom? By Joseph. "When I was at home," thought he, "my father would place before me any goodly portion [of food] that he saw, which made my brothers envious. Now I give thanks to Thee that I am at my ease." Said the Holy One to him: "Empty words! By thy life, I will incite the she-bear against thee."

Another comment: [Joseph said to himself] "My father was
tried, and my grandfather was tried, but I am not put to the test."
Said God to him: "By thy life! I will try thee even more than
them." (Genesis Rabbah 87:4)

The basis for both comments must be explained. In biblical
Hebrew, the word "debarim" can mean either "events," "things,"
"words," or "thoughts." The phrase "And it came to pass after these
things" usually means, "sometime later," but occasionally, the words
are midrashically interpreted as "And it came to pass after these
words," or ". . . after these thoughts." Such a device allows the
Midrash to fill in the biblical text with dialogue or monologue. In this
case, Joseph is made to have particular thoughts about his life. In
essence, he boasts that his life is too good and he would like more
challenges. To the Rabbis, such a sentiment amounted to asking for
trouble, and therefore God was glad to comply. The moral behind
their statement is still observed today: Don't say things are good unless
you want your luck to change, and never wish that life could be harder.

The biblical text next presents Mrs. Potiphar's words of seduction,
which in Hebrew are only two words (and in English only three): "LIE
WITH ME!" (Genesis 39:7). After noting that such an approach is
not only immoral but uncouth, the Midrash quickly focuses on
Joseph's response.

BUT HE REFUSED, AND SAID UNTO HIS MASTER'S
WIFE: BEHOLD, MY MASTER, HAVING ME, KNOWETH
NOT WHAT IS IN THE HOUSE, AND HE HATH PUT ALL
THAT HE HATH INTO MY HAND; HE IS NOT GREATER
IN THIS HOUSE THAN I; NEITHER HATH HE KEPT
BACK ANY THING FROM ME BUT THEE, BECAUSE
THOU ART HIS WIFE. HOW THEN CAN I DO THIS
GREAT WICKEDNESS, AND SIN AGAINST GOD? (Gene-
sis 39:8-9)

The biblical text informs us straightaway that Joseph refused. Furthermore, the reasons behind his refusal are explicitly presented. (It should be noted that the cantillation mark traditionally associated with the Hebrew word for HE REFUSED in the verse occurs very rarely. Whoever assigned such a mark hundreds of years ago either wanted to emphasize Joseph's adamant refusal or wished to imply that Joseph may not have been as emphatic as we might think.) In the plain biblical context, Joseph appears to argue from a pragmatic perspective: namely, sleeping with Mrs. Potiphar would not be a good way to show gratitude to Mr. Potiphar. Nevertheless, the biblical text is perplexing because, at the end of his explanation, Joseph adds a theological dimension to his reasoning: if he sleeps with her he also will be sinning against God.

Such a statement leads the Rabbis to wonder: Is Joseph refusing for pragmatic or religious reasons, or might it be for both? Furthermore, how does Joseph come to be concerned with divine judgment, since his earlier behavior never reflects divine awareness? (Even when he initially succeeds in Potiphar's house, and the Bible declares that God is with Joseph, we never are told that Joseph is aware of such divine aid, although the Midrash prefers to see Joseph this way.)

In order to understand what, exactly, Joseph is thinking when he refuses the advances of Mrs. Potiphar, the Midrash attempts to understand various possible arguments, all based on Joseph's response, BEHOLD, MY MASTER (Genesis 39:8). As we will see, three different understandings of the term, MY MASTER, are presented in the Midrash:

BEHOLD, MY MASTER (or, LORD): He said to her: "I am afraid of the 'Behold, the man is become like one of us . . .' (Genesis 3:22). Adam violated but a light commandment, for which he was banished from the Garden of Eden; how much more then for a grave offense!"

Another interpretation of BEHOLD, MY MASTER: "I am afraid of my father," [Joseph told her]. "Because Reuben lay with

Bilhah [Jacob's concubine], he was deprived of the birthright and it was given to me. Shall I harken to thee and be degraded from my birthright?"

Another interpretation of BEHOLD, MY MASTER: "I am afraid of my master," [Joseph told her]. "Then I will kill him," she urged. "Is it not enough that I should be counted in the company of adulterers, but I am to be counted among murderers too!" he replied. "Yet if you desire this thing, BEHOLD MY MASTER—there he is before thee!" Rabbi Isaac observed: The milk of white goats and the milk of black goats are one and the same! (*Genesis Rabbah* 87:5)

In classic fashion, the Midrash manages to stretch out two Hebrew words (three in English) into a whole range of possible moral arguments. Since the phrase, BEHOLD, MY MASTER, features the word *ADONI* in Hebrew, and this word is close to the name of God, *ADONAI*, the Midrash begins by saying that, all along, Joseph refused to sin because of God (and not because of his earthly master). Furthermore, according to the Midrash, the word BEHOLD reminds Joseph of an earlier scene in Genesis where Adam and Eve sin and God more or less declares, "Behold, Adam (and Eve) have eaten of the forbidden fruit and must be punished." Joseph reasons that, if their punishment was exile, certainly commiting adultery would lead to an even more severe divine punishment. Although the reader might applaud Joseph for reaching this conclusion, it is also clear that his motive is not too morally sophisticated. His basic motivation is simply so he will not be punished. (Note: The notion that Joseph is aware of what God did to Adam and Eve is not troublesome to the Rabbis. They liked to imagine that the earlier stories were passed down to the later generations. Likewise, in his "midrashic" novel, *Joseph and His Brothers*, Thomas Mann often has his biblical characters remember the ancient tales.)

It is possible, however, that when Joseph declares, BEHOLD, MY MASTER, he is remembering his father, who in effect still controls his behavior. Joseph knows that his father would never forgive him for commiting adultery, and so therefore he refuses to please Mrs. Potiphar. Once again, the Midrash presents Joseph as a young man who acts appropriately, but the motivation is not too morally sophisticated.

The final reading of BEHOLD, MY MASTER in effect presents Joseph as simply being afraid of the power of Potiphar. When Mrs. Potiphar suggests killing him, Joseph understands that Egyptian law will only punish him more severely. The midrashic comment concludes by removing a comma from the phrase, making Joseph declare not "Remember that my master will find out" but simply "If you want to sleep with someone, remember my master"—sleep with *him*. Rabbi Isaac (probably Isaac Nappaha of the third and fourth centuries in Palestine) then adds the gratuitous observation that Potiphar should be able to satisfy his wife as well as Joseph (unless he is a eunuch, as an earlier midrashic comment suggested).

The Midrash is clever in its trifold understanding of Joseph's motivations for refusing, but the three motivations are actually one: Joseph refuses out of fear, whether we call it fear of God, father, or boss. Hence, although Joseph does refuse, his moral reasoning is not sophisticated. He does not invoke philosophical support for his choice, hence leading one to think that if he could get away with it, Joseph would gladly say yes. All in all, such a portrayal of Joseph is consistent with *Genesis Rabbah's* view of Joseph. Although he might do the right thing, he is far from a perfect role model of virtue; certainly he is not yet "Joseph the Righteous."

It is also clear that Joseph does not effectively convince Mrs. Potiphar of his disinterest in being with her. The biblical text continues by declaring that Mrs. Potiphar spoke to Joseph daily of her passion. At this point, the Midrash chooses to respond to a question it assumes the biblical reader must be asking, namely: Is it not possible that Joseph *does* consent to sleep with Mrs. Potiphar? In order to respond, the Midrash resorts to a popular method of addressing such nagging concerns, that of the matron and her questions:

A matron asked Rabbi Jose: "Is it possible that Joseph, at seventeen years of age, with all the hot blood of youth, could act thus [refusing to be with Mrs. Potiphar]?" Thereupon he [Rabbi Jose] produced the Book of Genesis and read the stories of Reuben [who sleeps with his father's concubine] and Judah [who sleeps with his daughter-in-law]. If Scripture did not suppress anything in the case of these, who were older and in their father's home [actually, Judah was not], how much the more in the case of Joseph, who was younger and on his own. (*Genesis Rabbah* 87:6)

Rabbi Jose (as we have seen before—in Chapter 1—Rabbi Jose Ben Halafta often debated Roman matrons) responds to the matron by arguing that if Joseph had sinned, the Bible would have reported it, since it reports the misdeeds of Joseph's brothers (not to mention the faults of all its protagonists, from Adam and Eve onward). The question of the matron does not so easily disappear, however, because the Bible itself makes it difficult to dismiss an intimation of Joseph's temptation. Not only is it logical to assume that the young, warm-blooded Joseph was tempted by Mrs. Potiphar; his status as a hero is heightened if the temptation is genuine. Early post-biblical retellings of this story like to portray Joseph as a superhuman who does not think twice about refusing Mrs. Potiphar. But *Genesis Rabbah* prefers to present a Joseph who is sorely tempted to comply, especially after the daily pressure placed upon him.

Beyond these concerns, there is another problem occupying the Rabbis. If Joseph is completely innocent, they ask, then why is he punished by being sent to jail? The Rabbis of the Midrash believed—as Joseph will come to understand—that nothing happens without divine providence. Therefore, when Joseph is later punished by Potiphar, it would not make theological sense if Joseph were innocent. Earlier, we saw how the Midrash implied Joseph's culpability when his primping leads to the notice of Mrs. Potiphar. Now, at the climax of the story between Joseph and Mrs. Potiphar, the Rabbis go even further in implying Joseph's sinful role in the affair.

In the biblical text we read:

AND IT CAME TO PASS ON A CERTAIN DAY, WHEN HE
WENT INTO THE HOUSE TO DO HIS WORK, AND
THERE WAS NONE OF THE MEN OF THE HOUSE
THERE WITHIN, THAT SHE CAUGHT HIM BY HIS GAR-
MENT, SAYING: "LIE WITH ME." AND HE LEFT HIS
GARMENT IN HER HAND, AND FLED, AND GOT HIM
OUT. (Genesis 39:11-12)

As we will see, the Midrash will begin its commentary by interpreting the significance of the phrases "A CERTAIN DAY" and "TO DO
HIS WORK." Although one might read such statements as casual
observations, designed to give the impression that it was an ordinary
day, the Midrash chooses to see a correspondence between the fact
that it is a "certain"—or special—day and that Joseph is still doing his
"work"—a term which may conceal an ulterior motive.

AND IT CAME TO PASS ON A CERTAIN DAY, WHEN HE
WENT INTO THE HOUSE TO DO HIS WORK. Rabbi
Judah said: On that day there was a celebration in honor of the
Nile; everyone went to see it, but he [Joseph] went into the
house to cast up his master's accounts.
      Rabbi Nehemiah said: It was a day of a theatrical perfor-
mance, which all flocked to see, but he went into the house to
cast up his master's accounts.
      Rabbi Samuel ben Nachman said: TO DO HIS WORK is
meant literally [i.e., he had a sexual liason in mind], but that
AND THERE WAS NOT A MAN—on examination he did
not find himself a man, for as Rabbi Samuel said: The bow was
drawn but it relaxed, as Scripture later says [about Joseph]: "And
his bow returned in strength" (Genesis 49:24). (Genesis Rabbah
87:7)

Once again, the Midrash presents us with a panel discussion, conducted by three distinguished rabbis. The first two, Rabbi Judah and Rabbi Nehemiah (both of third century Palestine), take a more positive view of Joseph's motives: Either the certain, special day was a pagan Nile festival (which fits in with the Egyptian context) or a theatrical performance (which reflects the Roman environment of the midrashic authors). Joseph, being a good Jewish boy, not only stays away from such idolotrous and/or frivolous activities; he also uses the time to work even harder for his master. (It is no wonder the Rabbis make Joseph an accountant, since his business acumen will be obvious later in the biblical story, when he controls the economy of the country.)

The comment of Rabbi Samuel comes as somewhat of a shock, although the Midrash has slowly been leading up to it. According to him, Joseph planned to finally give in to Mrs. Potiphar. The celebrated day was obviously picked because no servants would be around and Mrs. Potiphar, presumably "sick" (or better, lovesick), would be alone. Nevertheless, as Joseph prepares to consumate his own lust, something happens to make him change his mind. The Midrash cleverly alludes to Jacob's eventual blessing for Joseph, which here is interpreted as a declaration of Joseph's moral strength, even while his sexuality is weakened.

Why does Joseph have second thoughts? The Midrash continues by providing the theory of Rabbi Huna, the fourth century Palestinian sage (taught in Rabbi Mattena's name):

He saw his father's face, at which his blood cooled. (*Genesis Rabbah* 87:7)

All of a sudden, argues Rabbi Huna, Joseph remembers his father, and by extension, the dreams of his youth. He recalls that his life has been set aside for something special, and his immediate gratification may very well place his entire mission in jeopardy. The reader already knows that if Joseph succumbs to Mrs. Potiphar, and Potiphar finds out, then Joseph will be killed, and all the divine plans for Joseph and his brothers and the eventual exodus from Egypt and the giving of Torah will come to naught. What is incredible is that Joseph somehow intuits this fact before it is too late. Joseph overcomes his passions, conquers the urge to sin, and thereby earns the title, "Joseph the Virtuous." Although the biblical tale of Joseph is far from complete at this point, the Midrash sees this event as the climax of Joseph's development. From this point onward, Joseph will excel based not only on his talents and good looks, but also because of the spiritual growth fostered by his passing this test of temptation. Even the subsequent prison term will not dampen Joseph's spirits; such is the power of righteousness.

The Rabbis of the Midrash saw Joseph as a role model for themselves. By overcoming temptation, he was fulfilling the ancient declaration of the sage Ben Zoma: "Who is strong? One who overcomes temptation." (*Mishna Avot* 4:1) The Rabbis understood that the lure of sexual transgression was not something to take lightly. (The appendix offers a brief narrative from the Talmud that masterfully presents the challenges that they faced.)

When Joseph is placed in prison after being accused by Mrs. Potiphar for harrassing *her*, the Midrash is careful to remind us that his punishment reflects minor transgressions that Joseph has made (such as vanity) but nothing like the charges against him.

AND JOSEPH'S MASTER TOOK HIM, AND PUT HIM INTO THE PRISON (Genesis 39:20). "I know that you are innocent," he [Potiphar] assured him, "but [I must do this] lest a stigma fall upon my children." (*Genesis Rabbah* 87:9)

The unstated but obvious message of Potiphar's remark is that, had Joseph really been guilty, death would have been the punishment. Even so, Joseph should consider himself lucky; he may have become a successful slave, but he has few rights, save what his master allows him. If we think of Joseph as a victim of sexual harrassment, we can

understand the pain that such modern victims must feel, especially
when colleagues of the perpetrator privately recognize the person's
guilt but refuse to make their concerns public. Potiphar's rationale is
no different than the cowardly reasons given today.
We next read that the prison warden is pleased with Joseph's
service. The Midrash cannot resist imagining a confrontation between Mrs. Potiphar and Joseph in jail.

... AND THE KEEPER OF THE PRISON COMMITTED
TO JOSEPH'S HANDS ALL THE PRISONERS . . . (Genesis
39:25 f.). Rabbi Huna said in Rabbi Hana's name: His service
was pleasing to his master [the prison keeper]: whenever he went
out, he would wash the cups, lay the tables, and make the beds.
She [Potiphar's wife] would taunt him, "See how I have made
you suffer! By your life, I will persecute you in other ways too." To
which he would reply, "[The Lord] Executeth justice for the per-
secuted" (Psalms 146:7). "I will have your food rations cut
down"—"He giveth bread to the hungry" (ibid.) was his reply. "I
will have you put in chains"—"The Lord looseth those who are
bound" (ibid.). "I will make you bent and bowed"—"The Lord
raiseth up them that are bowed down" (Psalms 146:8). "I will blind
you"—"The Lord openeth the eyes of the blind" (ibid.). How far did
she go? Said Rabbi Huna in Rabbi Aha's name: She went as far
as to place an iron fork under his neck so that he should have to
lift up his eyes and look at her. Yet in spite of that he would not
look at her. Thus it is written, "His feet they hurt with fetters, his
person was laid in iron" (Psalms 105:18). (Genesis Rabbah 87:10)

It appears that, according to the Midrash, a strange transformation
has occured within Joseph. Although he has not lost his drive to
succeed, his overcoming temptation has given him a new faith in
God's power. Although we might applaud such a transformation, the
midrashic characterization of Joseph also loses some of its luster.
Instead of a Joseph who is all too human, we have a Scripture-citing

fundamentalist, a superhuman Joseph. (Midrashically speaking, it is not a problem for Joseph to be quoting from Psalms, even though they would not be written for centuries. The Rabbis liked to envision their biblical heroes as well-versed in the Bible.) If the pre-prison Joseph was characterized by his vanity and charisma, the new Joseph is appropriately respectful of the dangerous ways of his past. Unfortunately, the new Joseph is also less fascinating. Perhaps it is for this reason that *Genesis Rabbah* seems to lose interest in Joseph after this point. Although there will be many more comments on the story, in comparison to the earlier material, the focus is certainly far less intense. It is almost as if Joseph, having conquered his sexual temptation, is now on auto-pilot, a righteous man who provides a good moral example but whose behavior has little relevance to human beings not endowed with his super strength.

Despite this fact, however, as we will see in the following chapter, there are still many rewarding insights which the Midrash will glean from the dramatic confrontation between Joseph and his brothers.

Chapter 4

Joseph Tests His Brothers

The poet A. R. Ammons once observed that, in every work of literature, "a world [comes] into being about which any statement, however revelatory, is a lessening." Such a sentiment may be thought by readers of the Midrash when it comes to the dramatic encounters between Joseph and his brothers. After all, how could any interpretive text improve upon the Bible's portrayal of the poignant soul-searching that plagues Joseph, now the viceroy of Egypt? There is a stark immediacy in such verses as, "Joseph saw his brethren, and he knew them, but made himself strange unto them . . ." (Genesis 42:7). Midrashic commentary, so helpful in clearing up textual confusion, easily appears as gratuitous in such scenes, like uninvited guests at a family reunion.

Nevertheless, in the chapters that relate Joseph's treatment of his brothers, there is one major question which the Midrash must address: Why does Joseph seemingly mistreat his brothers? Is "Joseph the Righteous" vengeful? And how do we explain Joseph's choice not to immediately contact his father and thereby relieve his grief? When Joseph first meets his brothers he quickly accuses them of spying, but nowhere do we read of their suspicious behavior. Is Joseph simply being nasty, or does he have a higher motive? Clearly, the Midrash would like to see Joseph,

45

having passed the test with Mrs. Potiphar, act like a righteous person. The task of the Midrash, without undercutting the beauty and drama of the biblical text, is to reassure the reader that Joseph has learned his lessons and is not reverting to his earlier vain and spoiled self.

After placing his brothers in jail for three days, Joseph convenes them and tells them to take food back to Canaan with his blessing, as long as they leave one of their brothers behind. In the meantime, the brothers are to return to Egypt with the youngest brother, Benjamin. Upon hearing this command, the brothers begin speaking in Hebrew, unaware that Joseph can understand them. They openly admit their guilt in selling Joseph into slavery and Joseph is so affected by their admission that he turns away and cries. When he returns, he takes Simeon and has him put in chains in front of the brothers. On the surface, it appears that Joseph's bitter memories lead him to exact revenge, but consider how the Midrash interprets Joseph's act:

AND HE [JOSEPH] TURNED HIMSELF ABOUT FROM THEM, AND WEPT; AND HE RETURNED TO THEM AND SPOKE TO THEM, AND TOOK SIMEON FROM AMONG THEM, AND BOUND HIM BEFORE THEIR EYES (Genesis 42:24). Rabbi Haggai commented in Rabbi Isaac's name: Only before their eyes did he bind them, but as soon as they left, he brought him out, gave him to eat and drink, and bathed and anointed him." (*Genesis Rabbah* 91:9)

Rabbi Haggai (a fourth century Palestinian sage) teaches that Joseph selects the brother he might hate most (for according to midrashic tradition, Simeon put him in the pit) but only *pretends* to persecute him. Joseph is not genuinely angry; he is putting on a show. (It has been pointed out by Robert Alter that his selection of Simeon is also strategically astute, since now Simeon and Levi, who usually plot together, will be separated.)

When Joseph's brothers eventually return with Benjamin, the stage is set for them to give Benjamin to Joseph. By means of the cup hidden in Benjamin's bag, Joseph makes it relatively easy for them to give him up. At this point in the biblical narrative, it becomes clear even without the help of the Midrash that Joseph's motive is ethically just: he wants to see if his brothers truly are repentant for selling Joseph into slavery. And when Judah, the most righteous of the brothers (except for Joseph, of course) approaches to sacrifice his own freedom in return for Benjamin, Joseph knows that his brothers have passed the test. He therefore is ready to reveal himself; he can be Joseph again.

THEN JOSEPH COULD NOT REFRAIN HIMSELF BE-FORE ALL THEM THAT STOOD BY HIM; AND HE CRIED: "CAUSE EVERY MAN TO GO OUT FROM ME." AND THERE STOOD NO MAN WITH HIM, WHILE JOSEPH MADE HIMSELF KNOWN UNTO HIS BRETH-REN. (Genesis 45:1)

Most biblical readers would be too caught up in the drama of the event to question the astuteness of Joseph at this moment. Nevertheless, the Midrash records a conversation regarding Joseph's behavior.

THEN JOSEPH COULD NOT REFRAIN HIMSELF . . . AND HE CRIED: CAUSE EVERY MAN TO GO OUT FROM ME. Rabbi Hama ben Rabbi Hanina and Rabbi Samuel ben Nahmani discussed this. Rabbi Hama ben Rabbi Hanina said: Joseph did not act prudently, for had one of them kicked him, he would have died on the spot.
Rabbi Samuel ben Nahmani said: He acted rightly and prudently. He knew the righteousness of his brethren and reasoned: "Heaven forfend! My brothers are not to be suspected of bloodshed." (Genesis Rabbah 93:9)

At stake is more than a discussion of the wisdom of Joseph's sending away his bodyguards. Rabbi Samuel stresses that Joseph is capable not only of forgiving his brothers; he also has faith in *their* ability to grow. Having passed his test, he has decided to reward his brothers with love and faith. Joseph's struggles lead him not only to value the power of self-transformation for himself; he now believes in the goodness of those who had sought to harm him. Clearly, Joseph has made peace not only with his past, but also with his future. Later, when he tells his brothers not to be afraid (of Joseph's anger), because God was behind all that occurred, Joseph is not retreating into what we moderns would call fundamentalism. He does not abdicate personal responsibility. He knows too well that we never know how our choices will affect the future and that therefore we must always strive to be righteous, with limited understanding of what we do. But beyond logic lies the realm of the divine plan, and at times the most "reasonable" response is to know that God is behind the inexplicable. Such a realization is not a retreat from reason or responsibility. As the philosopher Soren Kierkegaard would call it, it is a "leap of faith." We do not reject our belief in the divine because such belief cannot be scientifically proven; rather, we recognize that our capacity to reason itself is limited. Beyond such reason is the power of the divine, mysterious but no less real.

As we have seen, Joseph tests his brothers, but he also must pass his own test. Having earned the title "righteous" for himself when he does not succumb to sexual temptation, he must now learn to see the righteousness in others, even in his hated brothers. By recognizing their *teshuva*—repentance—he practices the highest act of *tsedaka*—righteousness. In a sense, Joseph makes not only a leap of faith but, as Abraham Joshua Heschel described it, a "leap of action" as well. His faith in the goodness of his brothers must be shown as well as felt.

After the climactic revelation and reunion, the biblical narrative veers away from Joseph and once again focuses on his father, Jacob. Nevertheless, Joseph's righteousness continues to have a strong presence in the Bible, even after he is dead. The final chapter of this book will explore this significant legacy of Joseph. As we will see, in order to examine this legacy, we will consult another midrashic compilation which adheres to the Book of Exodus.

Chapter 5

The Legacy of Joseph

Like Marley's ghost in A *Christmas Carol*, Joseph turns up long after he is laid to rest. Unlike the Dickens character, however, Joseph's afterlife is not a ghost story. Rather, his bones—and nothing more (at least in a physical sense)—are strangely immortal. For some reason, ancient interpreters of the Joseph story saw great significance in having the remains of Joseph play an important role in the Exodus narrative. Hence, while Abraham, Isaac, and Jacob are revered as the Patriarchs, Joseph the Righteous is praised for the "survival" of his skeleton.

Unlike later Jewish texts, the Bible does not relate a strong view of the afterlife. When characters die, we read that they are "gathered to their people," or as King David says, "go the way of all the earth." The vital concern is not what happens to the soul after death but whether or not the body is treated with respect. For the ancient readers of the Bible, Joseph was too righteous for his bones to rest eternally in Egypt. Therefore, when he makes his brothers swear that his bones will one day be returned to the Promised Land, the fulfillment of this promise in the Book of Exodus is of great interest. One very early interpretive source, Ben Sira, even limits his interest in Joseph to one line: "There has not been born another man like Joseph; yea, his remains were taken care of" (Ben Sira 49:15).

As we will see, the Rabbis who composed the great midrashic works on the Bible were also interested in the remains of Joseph and their importance in the Exodus narrative. Since the Exodus story is not found in the Book of Genesis, Midrash *Genesis Rabbah* is not the source for finding rabbinic commentary on the return of Joseph's bones. Therefore, we will turn to an early midrashic compilation on the Book of Exodus, *Mekhilta deRabbi Ishmael*, hereafter referred to as *Mekhilta*, or the Midrash.

In the conclusion, more will be said of this Midrash. For now, it is only important to know that although this collection was edited a couple of hundred years before *Genesis Rabbah*, and obviously relates to another biblical book, the methodology employed is not radically different. Since the Book of Exodus contains many laws, and Genesis does not, *Mekhilta* is primarily concerned with interpreting biblical law. Nevertheless, both *Genesis Rabbah* and *Mekhilta* also respond to narrative portions of Scripture, and here, generally speaking, the differences in style are not so pronounced.

To appreciate the rabbinic commentary on Joseph's bones, we begin by examining the charge of Joseph to his brothers, found in the last part of the Book of Genesis:

AND JOSEPH SAID UNTO HIS BRETHREN: I DIE; BUT GOD WILL SURELY REMEMBER YOU, AND BRING YOU UP OUT OF THIS LAND UNTO THE LAND WHICH HE SWORE TO ABRAHAM, TO ISAAC, AND TO JACOB. AND JOSEPH TOOK AN OATH OF THE CHILDREN OF ISRAEL, SAYING: "GOD WILL SURELY REMEMBER YOU, AND YE SHALL CARRY UP MY BONES FROM HENCE." SO JOSEPH DIED, BEING A HUNDRED AND TEN YEARS OLD. AND THEY EMBALMED HIM, AND HE WAS PUT IN A COFFIN IN EGYPT. (Genesis 50:24–26)

After this mention of Joseph's request, the Bible says nothing until well into the Book of Exodus. Specifically, in chapter 13, when the Israelites have already left the chains of slavery and are on the way to the Sea of Reeds, we learn that "MOSES TOOK THE BONES OF JOSEPH WITH HIM; FOR HE [JOSEPH] HAD STRAITLY SWORN THE CHILDREN OF ISRAEL, SAYING: 'GOD WILL SURELY REMEMBER YOU; AND YE SHALL CARRY UP MY BONES AWAY HENCE WITH YOU'." (Exodus 13:19).

A casual reading of the biblical narrative might not raise any concerns. Joseph has his brothers swear that his remains will be returned to Canaan, and hundreds of years later, Moses carries out the wishes of Joseph. If we look more closely at the chain of events, however, some questions arise. First of all, why did the Israelites not return Joseph's bones immediately after he died (as in the case of Jacob)? Why is he embalmed and placed into a coffin in Egypt? Furthermore, when Joseph's remains are taken by the Israelites, why does Moses himself perform the task? One would think that, with all his other duties, a deputy could have been appointed.

Responding to the second question first, we might simply state that the biblical style reports that Moses took his bones in the same way that Pharaoh, we are told, makes ready his chariot (Exodus 14:6). In reality, neither man performed the task. We might also conclude that Moses, like many leaders today, had a problem delegating simple chores. As we will see, the Midrash provides a very different answer.

AND MOSES TOOK THE BONES OF JOSEPH WITH HIM (Exodus 13:19). This proclaims the wisdom and the piety of Moses. For all [the people of] Israel were busy with the booty while Moses busied himself with the duty of looking after the bones of Joseph. Of him Scripture says: "The wise in heart takes on duties" (Proverbs 10:8).

But how did Moses know where Joseph was buried? It is told that Serah, the daughter of Asher, survived from that generation and she showed Moses the grave of Joseph. She said to him:

The Egyptians put him into a metal coffin which they sunk in the Nile. So Moses went and stood by the Nile. He took a tablet of gold on which he engraved the Tetragrammaton [the four-letter name of God] and throwing it into the Nile, he cried out and said: "Joseph son of Jacob! The oath to redeem his children, which God swore to our father Abraham, has reached its fulfillment. If you come up, well and good. But if not, we shall be guiltless of your oath." Immediately Joseph's coffin came to the surface, and Moses took it. . . . (*Mekhilta, Beshallah*)

The Midrash begins by providing an answer to the question of why Moses himself takes Joseph's bones. Because the rest of the Israelites, too busy with taking the gold of their Egyptian neighbors (a fact which the Bible mentions), were not thinking of the oath. In other words, Moses' piety transcended that of his people. He alone had the sensitivity to worry about fulfilling Joseph's request.

In characteristic fashion, however, the Midrash raises more questions than it answers. For instance, why is Moses called "wise in heart" when he piously takes Joseph's bones? It would make more sense to call him pious or virtuous. Apparently, Moses must be more than kind in order to carry out his task. He must also use his wisdom in order to *locate* the bones of Joseph. The Midrash continues by explaining that Joseph's bones were not easy to find, for they had been thrown into the Nile, a fact which Scripture certainly never mentions.

The Midrash does not explain why the Egyptians put Joseph into a metal casket and threw him into the Nile, but it does provide a theory for how Moses discovers that Joseph's bones are in the river. Serah, an Israelite mentioned in the Book of Genesis, also appears in a geneology in the Book of Numbers. Instead of concluding, as we might, that a different Serah is mentioned, the Midrash assumes that the same woman has lived for hundreds of years and therefore knows where Joseph was buried. Then, Moses, taking matters into his own hands, succeeds in raising Joseph.

In order to answer the first question, namely, why Joseph's body was not buried in Canaan immediately following his death, there is the intimation that the Egyptians did not want Joseph's body leaving Egypt; hence they threw his coffin in the Nile. A non-rabbinic but ancient Jewish interpretive text, the Book of Jubilees, explains that Joseph's remains were not taken to Canaan because a war had broken out between Canaan and Egypt, and therefore the transfer was not possible. Another ancient text, the Testament of Simeon, also mentions such a war. Furthermore, it explicitly states that the wizards of Egypt feared the departure of Joseph's bones; therefore, they purposefully hid them. (They rightly predicted that when Joseph's bones left, so would the Israelites.)

The Midrash we have been studying, Mekhilta, continues by providing a related version of the story, in which Joseph's coffin is not thrown into the Nile but hidden in the Pyramids. The Midrash concludes by explaining what happened to Joseph's bones for the forty years when the Israelites were in the Wilderness, and for the time in the Promised Land until Joshua buries his bones in Shechem.

Furthermore, the coffin of Joseph went alongside the ark of the Eternal (which held the Ten Commandments). And the nations would say to the Israelites: What are these two chests? And the Israelites would say to them: The one is the ark of the Eternal, and the other is a coffin with a body in it. The nations would then say: What is the importance of this coffin that it should go alongside of the ark of the Eternal? And the Israelites would say to them: The one lying in this coffin has fulfilled that which is written on what lies in that ark. . . . (Mekhilta Beshallah)

For the rabbis of the Midrash, no remark could more greatly reflect the respect they have for the legacy of Joseph. Here was a man, they say, who lived a life filled with anguish and temptation, but who transcended these challenges. He did not grow bitter. He did not succumb to the evils around him. Not as a superhero did he succeed but as a man of flesh and blood. Joseph the Righteous, Joseph the Virtuous, is heralded as the living embodiment of the Ten Commandments, and by extension, the entire Torah.

And so, in the Book of Joshua, Joseph's remains are finally laid to rest in Shechem, the place where, according to tradition, his journey started when he met a man (or angel) wandering in the field and ready to tell him where his brothers waited. Hundreds of years later Joseph returns home, and thousands of years later his legacy remains with us. The genius of the Bible is that it gives us not only laws but also people whose lives reflect the struggle to live by those laws. The art of the Midrash is its ability to highlight the amazing accomplishments of our biblical heroes. Although some post-biblical interpretation makes characters such as Joseph into stock figures of virtue, *Genesis Rabbah* in particular presents a human Joseph who, by his fortitude and innate goodness, earns the title "Joseph the Righteous" and the singular comparison with the Torah itself. Our task as human beings is to reflect the success of Joseph. Even if we fail, our humanity will be enriched by the noble example that Joseph gives us. Such is the legacy of Joseph.

Conclusion: An
Overview of the Midrash

It is hoped that the preceding chapters have offered an inductive
introduction to the genre of midrash which, by definition, must
transcend any attempt to define midrash here. I firmly believe that our
experience in reading these texts will lead us to an understanding far
more profound than what a descriptive summary can do. Nevertheless, in the next few pages we will investigate the primary characteristics of the genre of midrash. Some of the books mentioned in the
bibliography which follows (see For Further Study) also provide excellent introductions to the nature of ttis literary and religious genre.

As was mentioned in the introduction, the word *midrash* can
either refer to the process of interpreting biblical texts or to specific
works which contain such interpretations. The focus in the book
has been on one such work, *Genesis Rabbah*, but the process that
this Midrash reflects is found in all midrashic collections (although
such collections are quite diverse in matters of style and attitude
toward Scripture).

The word *midrash* first appears in the Bible in two chronologically
late passages (2 Chronicles 13:22 and 24:27), and may refer to particular works of interpretation. Nevertheless, the verb from which the

name is derived is found throughout the Bible, and is usually understood to mean "to investigate." For the last two thousand years, the word has been used synonymously for "study" (hence the name, *bet-ha-midrash*, the "house of study"). Therefore, the word need not refer to actual interpretations of Scripture. Nevertheless, in a technical sense, from Late Antiquity until now, this has been the essential meaning of the word.

Midrash, or the interpretation of Scripture, developed as a response to Scripture itself. In other words, the very act of relating stories and laws (which is the fundamental task of the Bible) inspires the asking of questions. For example, when we read that Cain killed his brother Abel, we want to know why the two argued and how Abel was killed. The Bible does not provide this information, and therefore the process of midrash is required. Obviously, such a need is not limited to narrative portions of the Bible. When, in the Book of Exodus, the laws *(mitzvot)* are given at Mount Sinai, the Midrash is needed to explain the laws and adapt them to changes in contemporary life. For instance, the Fourth Commandment tells us to "remember the Sabbath day and keep it holy," but the details for such remembrance are not provided (beyond a few general prohibitions such as "do not work"). It is up to the Midrash (and its sister work, the Talmud) to provide a detailed interpretation of the significance of such laws.

Modern scholarship in the field of midrash often adopts the rabbinical categorization of midrashic works into *midrash halakhah* (law) and *midrash aggadah* (lore). Hence, midrashic compilations which feature interpretations of biblical laws are called halakhic because they focus on the legal ramifications of Scripture (and how we must change our understanding as society changes). A classic example is the biblical law which mandates that, if a person puts out the eye of another, then that person, too, must lose an eye. In the midrashic and talmudic interpretations of this law, it is made clear that a figurative understanding of Scripture is required: the instigator does not actually lose an eye but must make some financial restitution.

With regard to *midrash aggadah*, narrative portions are discussed and analyzed by the Rabbis in a fashion not completely unlike modern literary criticism's relation to such primary texts. In addition to the example of Cain and his brother, a classic opportunity for such midrashic activity is the Binding of Isaac story (chapter 22 of the Book of Genesis). This brief tale is investigated in awesome detail in various midrashic compilations.

Despite the utility in dividing midrashic literature into two camps, halakhic and aggadic, there is a fundamental problem with this approach: the midrashic compilations themselves are almost never completely one or the other. In the period when these classic works were edited (ca. 200 C.E. to 800 C.E.) the Rabbis were not rigidly divided into halakhic and aggadic spheres. Sometimes, as in the case of Rabbi Akiba, they were experts in both fields. Furthermore, because even a book like Leviticus, which is primarily legal (or at least cultic) in scope, contains some narrative material, the corresponding Midrash will also offer aggadic insights. Perhaps, when it comes to midrash, it is best to be aware of the distinction between *aggadah* and *halakhah*, but in classifying such material we should not be more rigid than were the ancient Rabbis.

Modern scholars also differentiate between exegetical midrash (i.e., interpreting the biblical text) and homiletical midrash (i.e., preaching on the biblical text). The former term implies that the Rabbi who is creating a midrash seeks to understand the contextual meaning of Scripture, while the latter term suggests that the Rabbi has a message to deliver and is using Scripture to support his argument. Although we can see both processes at work in many midrashic collections, including *Genesis Rabbah*, a more than general distinction is problematic. First of all, it is almost never clear what the ancient Rabbi meant by the "contextual meaning" of Scripture, since such an approach is never truly objective. Furthermore, the sermonic material that the midrashic collections preserve do not reflect actual rabbinic presentations, but later literary creations. Hence, editors with exegetical concerns, as well as preachers interested in finding the "contextual meaning," at times will produce "exegetical" midrash in "homiletical" settings. The complexity of such issues is a good reason to be careful when using the terms exegetical and homiletical for describing midrashic compilations.

A third classification system divides midrashic compilations chronologically. Hence, the earliest works, such as the commentary to the Book of Exodus entitled "Mekhilta deRabbi Ishmael" (which we looked at in the previous chapter), are called "tannaitic," referring to the first two centuries of the Common Era. Later works, including Genesis Rabbah, are called "amoraic." The problem with this classification is that later works often contain earlier material and therefore we might speak of "tannaitic" portions of Genesis Rabbah, a collection of the "amoraic" period. There is also another problem: statements attributed to earlier Rabbis may actually come from later Sages, thereby calling into question the entire dating system based on attributions. (Putting contemporary ideas into the mouths of venerated teachers of old was a popular way to gain authority.) As we see, once again the complexities of such a classification approach threaten to outweigh any benefits.

It seems to me that, instead of concerning themselves with classifications, most modern readers of midrash should focus on a more conceptual level, namely: what is the midrashic text trying to accomplish? What issues are the Rabbis addressing and what literary techniques do they employ? We know that the ancient authors of midrash, unlike most of us, believed that every word of Scripture was divine, either directly dictated by God (as in the Torah) or inspired by God (as in everything else). The belief in divine authorship provided the Rabbis with a focus for their life; even in exile and long after the end of prophecy, the Bible provided them with a link to God. However, with such a link came a heavy burden of responsibility: the Rabbis needed to see how Scripture related to their contemporary concerns. For example, for the authors of Genesis Rabbah, the biblical Joseph becomes a model of rabbinic righteousness. His experience in an alien culture, his ability to conquer temptation, and his spiritual development are understood in rabbinic terms. *Mekhilta* preserves this approach, too—hence the statement that Joseph's life reflected the Ten Commandments.

In the case of Joseph, interpreting his life in light of the rabbinic period was relatively easy. At times the task of making the Bible relevant for the Rabbis and their era was quite daunting. For instance, the laws of ritual sacrifice which fill the Book of Leviticus are discussed in great detail in the early midrashic compilation on Leviticus (entitled *Sifra*). A few hundred years later, however, it is clear that such an approach to Leviticus is unrealistic, since the Temple and the sacrificial cult have been destroyed and extinct for centuries (and won't be resumed in the foreseeable future). The result of this transformation is a midrashic work, *Leviticus Rabbah*, that labors to find ethical (and often even universal) lessons in the Book of Leviticus.

In order to approach Leviticus in such a way, *Leviticus Rabbah* employs various literary techniques. A well-known example is the parable, or *mashal*, which in rabbinic context refers to a stock narrative (involving characters such as a king and his wife) that resonates with theological insights derived from Scripture. Other common strategies include word-plays, "misreadings" of biblical verses, and intertextual juxtapositions in which other books of the Bible are related to passages from Leviticus. (We saw a similar technique relating to Genesis in chapter three of this book.) In general, all of this activity is designed to re-examine the message of the biblical text and make it relevant to the issues of the day. Although the biblical text is sometimes wrenched out of context, the Rabbis respected the contextual integrity of the Bible. They simply believed that such attempts were permitted (and naturally foreseen) by God. As they liked to declare, the Torah has seventy faces (i.e., each verse has seventy possible interpretations).

Although our approach to Scripture may be different, I believe we can learn two valuable insights from the attitude of the ancient Rabbis. First, we can be inspired by their passion for Scripture. They believed in its redemptive force to shape their lives. We, in an era of so much doubt and confusion, could certainly use some of their passion, even if our assumptions when approaching the text are, for lack of a better term, more secular. At its heart, midrash is simply a way to heighten the power of the Bible in one's life, and such a process could greatly enhance our own spiritual development.

The second insight is found in the heterogeneous nature of midrash. As we have seen, "another opinion" is a common phrase in the texts we studied. It is likewise popular throughout midrashic literature. In general, the midrashic process values dissent (within boundaries, of course) and such a healthy approach should illuminate our own discussions concerning Scripture, spirituality, and everything we hold sacred.

In conclusion, let me say this: if, after reading this book, you are inspired to study midrash (or the Midrash) in more detail, that would be wonderful. If you are not interested, I would be disappointed, but only slightly. What concerns me much more is if you were inspired to study Scripture with more passion and interest. For this is the beauty of midrash: when it inspires us to (re)visit the transcendant realm of Torah, and when it (re)turns us toward the fundamental story of Judaism (as well as the foundation for two other great faiths). If this study of midrash inspires you to undertake such a challenge, then it has superbly succeeded, and the true treasure of midrash has been discovered.

Appendix

Temptation in the Talmud

Although the focus of this book has been on the midrashic process in general and on *Genesis Rabbah* and the Joseph story in particular, the rabbinic values reflected in midrash are also found in its sister text, the Talmud. Most people think of the Talmud as a corpus of Jewish legal discussion *(halakhah)*, but the Talmud also contains extensive interpretation of biblical narrative as well as tales about the Jewish people in general and the ancient Rabbis in particular (what we call *aggadah*).

These stories have not been taken too seriously by traditional readers of the Talmud. Usually they are appreciated for their ability to lighten up the usually dry tone of the text, but that is all. They certainly are not considered to be artistic. Nevertheless, many modern scholars have come to recognize the literary qualities of many of these tales. As in the midrashic passages studied throughout this book, such stories often reflect the important themes and values of our heritage. Furthermore, they are skillfully written in ways that avoid

---

I am indebted to Jonathan Cohen of Hebrew University for calling my attention to this story and its interpretive possibilities. My analysis is in part based on his reading and on the insights of Jonah Fraenkel, also of Hebrew University.

dogmatism, and like many passages in the midrash, they reward the close reader with rich insights into the human condition.

According to Aristotle, artistic creations must be ordered and measured properly; they cannot begin and end randomly. We might say they must reflect a balance between form and function. The following short story relates to an important theme of the Joseph story, that of overcoming temptation. As we will see, the tone of the tale is straightforward and, at first glance, the events may seem common. Nevertheless, a closer reading should reveal a more sophisticated and challenging portrait that incorporates true artistry in its presentation of the narrative.

Here is the tale (from the Babylonian Talmud, tractate *Sukkah* 52a):

> It is told of Abbaye
> That he heard a certain man say to a certain woman:
> "Come, let's walk down the road together."
> He (Abbaye) said (to himself): "I will walk (also), and part (prevent) them from doing forbidden things."
> He walked after them for a distance of three parsot through the country.
> When they parted, he heard them say (to each other):
> "The road has been long, but your company has been a pleasure."
> Abbaye said (to himself): "I could never have had the power to resist."
> He walked and leaned against the fence, feeling sorry (or sad).
> An old man came by and taught him:
> "The great ones are those that have the greater desires."

The narrative element of this story appears simple enough. A man named Abbaye overhears a presumably private conversation between another man and a woman. The man suggests to the woman that the two of them take a walk together. Abbaye decides to walk with them (or after them). After some time, he hears the couple part from each other. It is fair to surmise that most readers would not anticipate the concluding scene, in which Abbaye admits to himself that he could never have the power to resist (what, the text does not say). Finally, an old man teaches him that the greater the person, the greater the desire. This exceedingly short story certainly is not guilty of providing too much detail. We are not told what the characters look like, or even the names of two of them. We do not know about the scenery of the country or how the couple look at each other, or even how they speak to one another. Nevertheless, I believe that imbedded in this miniature tale are some profound insights into human nature, and only the careful reader will be able to recognize these teachings.

The best way to read this story is to ask a lot of questions, especially since so much narrative detail is left out (perhaps on purpose). For instance, in the first sentence, we are told that a certain man and woman decide to take a trip together. What does the appellation "certain" mean? Are these well-known members of the community, or do they represent everyman and everywoman? How does the certain man ask the certain woman to accompany him on the trip? Does his manner imply a lewd motive or a chivalrous one?

We know that, at this point in the story, the man may have a number of reasons for asking the woman to accompany him. Since we are not mindreaders, the actual reason eludes us. Nevertheless, we can observe the choice that Abbaye makes, and while we may learn little about the couple from this choice, we learn a lot about Abbaye. He decides to follow the couple in order to prevent them from doing "forbidden things" (obviously alluding to prohibited sex). Abbaye's view of human nature is apparently pessimistic (or realistic). Perhaps he knows something in particular about this certain man or woman, or perhaps he simply knows something about the human race.

We next learn that Abbaye follows the couple for a considerable distance through the country. Some scholars suggest that three parsot (or parasangs) is the equivalent of about ten miles. In addition, the Aramaic word for "country" actually refers to a reeded area near a body of water. Taking these facts into consideration, we have the following scenario: the couple wanders into an area which easily would conceal inappropriate behavior. The reeds also enable Abbaye to follow his couple without their noticing him. (Unless, of course, they actually do know that he is there.) Certainly the fact that Abbaye shadows them for such a long period of time attests to his stamina and zeal in protecting society's mores. (Unless, of course, he actually wants to see the couple engage in illicit activity.)

When Abbaye overhears them take leave from each other, they now speak together, implying that the couple are of one mind. In contrast, Abbaye seems to be inwardly divided. How else can we explain the disappointment he expresses (perhaps there is some relief mixed in)? On the one hand, Abbaye must be glad that nothing untoward has occurred; on the other hand, Abbaye's own moral strength has been questioned. He has understood that, despite his position of leadership (even if it is only self-proclaimed), Abbaye is all too human. When the old man finds him leaning against a fence (Abbaye is physically as weak as he is morally threatened), words of consolation are given to him. (It should be noted that the entire story in the Talmud is related in Aramaic—the basic language of the Talmud—but the words of the old man are rendered in Hebrew, as if they are an old proverb.)

What does the old man mean by his statement? How will Abbaye respond? These questions are not answered. Nevertheless, the basic message of the story becomes clear: Abbaye assumes that the couple are planning evil because he projects his own fantasies upon them. What he comes to learn after travelling "into the woods" (as in all good fairy tales) is that his personality is split between his will to do good and his impulse toward evil. His righteousness was concealing his own failings from him, surely a dangerous phenomenon for any leader. The ancient Rabbis recognized that sexual temptation leads to transgression, but so does righteousness when it is taken out of perspective. "Be not righteous overmuch," they exclaimed, as if speaking to Abbaye, who actually was a leader in fourth century Babylon. In the preceding book, the righteousness of Joseph has been considered in light of the midrashic understanding of Joseph's character. Although Joseph had a great deal to learn about the meaning of virtue, to his credit he is not guilty of too much virtue. Nevertheless, the rest of us may not be so fortunate. Abbaye's ordeal teaches us that morality and virtue have their own temptations, and that all of us have underlying human urges that must not be ignored. The measure of a person is not in the amount of temptation he is presented with, but in his ability to overcome it. This is the great triumph of Joseph and the sad realization of Abbaye.

Besides providing this important insight into human nature, our text also reflects a meeting of form and function. In its very presentation, the fundamental message of our inner-divisiveness is manifest. In other words, we can easily divide the story into two parts (excluding the preamble "It is told of Abbaye" and the last scene featuring the old man). Clearly, the first part consists of Abbaye's hearing the plans of the couple and following them into the woods. The second part begins when the couple part and ends with Abbaye's dejection. In addition, each of these two parts can be divided into four sections, as the above translation shows. The upshot of these divisions is that the story is divided into two equal parts, just as the couple are two who become one (in their minds), and Abbaye is one who is really two (in his mind).

Furthermore, there is a parallel between the two sections. In the first part, Abbaye thinks about the couple; in the latter part he thinks about himself. In an article, which in part deals with this story, Jonah Fraenkel* also points out some of the verbal assonances that are featured in order to draw comparisons between the characters. In general, the two-part division of the story reflects Abbaye's divided state of mind, and by extension, the challenge of each of us to bring into harmony our dual selves. Such is the challenge of temptation.

---

*Jonah Fraenkel, "The Structure of Talmudic Aggadic Stories [Hebrew]," in *Studies in Aggadah and Jewish Folklore*, ed. Issachar Ben-Ami and Joseph Dan (Jerusalem: Magnus, 1983), pp. 65–69).

For Further Study

The following material (in English and currently available) offers valuable (and, for the beginner, *accessible*) insights into the nature of midrash and/or the story of Joseph:

Alter, Robert. *The Art of Biblical Narrative.* New York: Basic Books, 1981.
　　Alter is a master in the art of closely reading biblical texts, and he also appreciates the fine insight of midrash.
Bader, Gershon. *The Encyclopedia of Talmudic Sages.* Trans. Solomon Katz. Northvale, NJ: Jason Aronson, 1993.
　　Extensive portraits of the major rabbinic contributors to the Midrash (as well as the Talmud) are provided.
Cohen, Norman J. *Self, Struggle and Change.* Woodstock, VT: Jewish Lights, 1995.
　　A personal reading of Genesis that draws on various midrashic traditions and a close reading of the biblical text.
Diamond, Eliezer. "The World of the Talmud." In *The Schocken Guide to Jewish Books,* ed. Barry W. Holtz, pp. 64–66. New York: Schocken, 1992.

The author provides an up-to-date (as of 1992) listing of available books in English that relate to midrash. Some of his suggested material may be too advanced for the beginning student.

Holtz, Barry. "Midrash." In *Back to the Sources*, ed. Barry Holtz, pp. 177–211. New York: Summit, 1984.

An excellent introduction to the nature of midrash. He also provides a valuable, although dated, bibliography. A more current list of books relating to midrash can be found in Holtz's *The Schocken Guide to Jewish Books* (see above, under Diamond).

Kugel, James. *In Potiphar's House: The Interpretive Life of Biblical Texts.* San Francisco: Harper, 1990. Kugel masterfully investigates the various motifs found in midrashic expansions of the Joseph narrative.

Mann, Thomas. *Joseph and His Brothers.* Trans. H. T. Lowe-Porte. New York: Knopf, 1944.

A literary masterpiece.

Neusner, Jacob. *Confronting Creation: How Judaism Reads Genesis.* Columbia, SC: University of Southern Carolina Press, 1991. A rather technical presentation of passages from *Genesis Rabbah.*

Niehoff, Maren. *The Figure of Joseph in Post-Biblical Jewish Literature.* Leiden: E. J. Brill, 1992.

This is a scholarly examination into three postbiblical treatments of the Joseph story, including the insights of *Genesis Rabbah.*

Porton, Gary G. *Understanding Rabbinic Midrash: Text and Commentary.* Hoboken, NJ: Ktav, 1985.

A somewhat scholarly overview of classic midrashic texts is provided. Not a book for beginners, but very useful as a guide for the more advanced student of midrash.

Stern, David. "Introduction." In *The Book of Legends: Sefer Ha-Aggadah,* ed. Hayim Nahman Bialik and Yehoshua Hana Ravnitzky. Trans. William G. Braude, pp. xvii-xxii. New York: Schocken, 1992.

Stern provides a concise portrait of the essential character of *aggadah.* The book itself is useful but the lack of commentary makes the material sometimes difficult to appreciate.

Stern, Jay. *What's a Nice God Like You Doing in a Place Like This?* New York: United Synagogue of America Commission on Jewish Education, 1987.

The author presents the midrashic process in a humorous light (as the title suggests). Although he expresses a clear love for the literature, his approach may be a little too glib for some readers.

Vizotzky, Burton L. *Reading the Book: Making the Bible a Timeless Text.* New York: Anchor, 1991.

The author presents midrashic traditions in a modern context.

Index

About the Author

Edwin Goldberg received rabbinic ordination and a doctorate in Hebrew literature from the Hebrew Union College–Jewish Institute of Religion. Rabbi Goldberg recently spent a year studying midrash and education at Hebrew University in Jerusalem. Currently, he is the associate rabbi at Temple Israel of Hollywood in Los Angeles, California, and also teaches at the University of Judaism in Los Angeles (in the Department of Continuing Education). He and his wife, Melanie, have two children, Joseph and Benjamin.

Printed in Great Britain
by Amazon